Independent Schools
Examinations Board

English Practice Exercises 13+
Answer Book
2nd Edition

Amanda Alexander
and Rachel Gee

Editor: Tom Cross

Independent Schools
Examinations Board

www.galorepark.co.uk

GALORE PARK

Published by Galore Park Publishing Ltd,
338 Euston Road, London, NW1 3BH
www.galorepark.co.uk

Text copyright Amanda Alexander and Rachel Gee 2013

The right of Amanda Alexander and Rachel Gee to be identified as the authors of this work has been asserted by them in accordance with sections 77 and 78 of the Copyright, Designs and Patents Act 1988.

Typesetting by Typetechnique
Printed by Charlesworth Press, Wakefield

ISBN: 978-1 907047 87 9

First edition published 2008, second edition published 2013

Details of other ISEB Revision Guides for Common Entrance, examination papers and Galore Park publications are available at www.galorepark.co.uk

About the authors

Amanda Alexander and Rachel Gee have extensive experience in teaching and managing in both state and private schools. They have a wealth of knowledge and considerable expertise in preparing children for English at 13+, which they bring to this book. They were the authors of the first edition of *English Practice Exercises 13+*.

Contents

Introduction

We hope that this answer book will be a useful tool for teachers and parents using and marking *English Practice Exercises 13+*.

The answer grid format to the reading texts, in Paper 1 Section A and Paper 2 Section A, is modelled on the ISEB mark schemes, as is the allocation of marks. We hope that this detailed analysis is a timesaver, with the key requirements of answers, main quotations and writing techniques all carefully identified. The answers are not totally prescriptive, as it is not possible to write a hard and fast mark scheme for English, unlike some other subjects. We acknowledge that children often discover the unusual and that teachers prefer the autonomy to mark in their own way.

The grids for marking the writing tasks in Paper 1 Section B and Paper 2 Section B contain the descriptors provided by the ISEB. We have included guidelines to aid the interpretation of the key words in those descriptors. The marking of writing is even more subjective than the marking of comprehension answers, but these grids provide a guide to the allocation of marks.

Teachers and parents may wish to use the sets of comprehension answers and guidance on writing expectations themselves. Alternatively, it may be preferable for candidates to have their own copy, at the marking stage, to have a better understanding of what is required and so improve their marks.

Paper 1 Section A:
Reading – Literary prose

1. *The Bookseller of Kabul* by Asne Seierstad

Level 1

Q		Answer	Mark	Additional guidance
1.	(a)	• 'sing at the top of their voices' (line 4) • 'Mansur has eaten the first packet of biscuits' (line 7) • 'drunk two Cokes' (lines 7–8) • 'He wants to scream and shout' (line 8) • 'and sticks his head out of the window' (lines 8–9) • '"Ouhhhhiiii! Here I come!"' (line 9)	2	two phrases/quotations needed for 2 marks
	(b)	• going to a New Year Festival • they are drinking Coke and Fanta and eating biscuits/on a sugar high • they feel free	2	one reason needed for 2 marks
2.	(a)	impressive snow-capped mountains rise up from the flat land in front of them	2	plain and mountains both to be referred to for 2 marks
	(b)	• 'rear up in the landscape like skeletons' (line 16) • the wrecked remains of villages seem like old bones dominating the scene/the scene is dominated by lifelessness/the scene seems to be occupied only by the dead and remains of houses/a scene that was full of life is now full of death	1 2	1 mark award up to 2 marks depending on detail given
3.		• 'potholed road' (line 20) – creates travelling difficulties • 'ruins' (line 21) – people's homes have been wrecked • 'rubble' (line 23) – people's homes have been wrecked and the landscape is changed • 'most mined place' (lines 24–25) – fear of hidden bombs/danger in going about everyday life	6	three quotations with explanations needed for 6 marks

		• 'Only the roads are safe.' (line 25) – have to walk in the road, which in itself is a danger/the women and children who collect firewood and water have to walk at the sides of the road		
4.	(a)	they laugh because: • the book is out of date and paints a wonderful picture of the landscape and is very different from the war-torn scene they now see • the information in the book contrasts with the reality • it would be ridiculous for children now to be selling flowers along the war-torn roads • there are no longer 'chains of pink tulips' (line 30) • trees/flowers no longer 'jostle for the attention of the traveller' (line 31), as sights of war more shocking/ overwhelming/obvious • 'bombs, rockets, a three-year drought and poisoned wells' (lines 33–34) – complete contrast with the book's description	3	up to 3 marks for understanding either one very detailed response or two responses in less detail
	(b)	• metaphor or personification • the trees are stubbornly/defiantly determined to survive against all the odds • the fact that they are rebels in a war zone is slightly ironic	1 2	up to 2 marks depending on detail of explanation
5.		• disgust: insensitive to laugh while area in ruins and people struggling to survive • deserve the fun: they are in high spirits because they feel their car (with music, Coke, Fanta and biscuits), protects them against the real world outside • justified: they are justified in having a day of fun in a war-torn zone	4	up to 4 marks for sensible reactions reward quality of response and empathy
TOTAL			**25**	

1. *The Bookseller of Kabul* by Asne Seierstad

Level 2

Q	Answer	Mark	Additional guidance
1.	the boys' behaviour: • 'The next morning, before dawn, they are off.' (lines 1–2) – they set off before dawn which suggests eagerness • 'Mansur has brought his treasure with him, a western cassette' (lines 4–5) – they play their favourite music and sing • 'Mansur has eaten the first packet of biscuits and drunk two Cokes.' (lines 7–8) – on a sugar high • 'He feels free.' (line 8) – he is enjoying a sense of freedom • 'He wants to scream and shout, and sticks his head out of the window.' (lines 8–9) – can hardly contain himself • '"Ouhhhhiiii! Here I come!"' (line 9) – shouting with excitement tense: • present tense – immediate/as if happening now/spontaneity/emphasises their enjoyment of the moment	4	up to 2 marks for evidence, in own words or quotation, and explanation up to 2 marks for recognition of tense and explanation of effect
2.	mountains: • metaphor: 'backdrop of the mighty snow-clad Hindu Kush mountains' (lines 13–14) – mountains are an impressive background to the scene • personification: 'mountains that proudly rise up to the sky' (line 14) – mountains seem to be pleased to be there/ self-important villages: • metaphor: 'rear up' (line 16) – loom up/ appear suddenly	6	mountains and villages to be referred to three techniques in total to be quoted, identified and explained

	• simile: 'rear up in the landscape like skeletons' (line 16) – the wrecked remains of villages seem like old bones with no life in or on them • alliteration: 'twisted tanks' (line 16) – sharp repeated 't' sound emphasises the tangled state of the tanks		
3.	boys: • young, sophisticated, healthy boys • within modern capsule of the car/ protected from the outside/feel safe/ enjoying each other's company local people: • unsophisticated, struggling for survival, poor man's ploughing is obstructed by wrecked tank • lonely in his/their work • children collect and carry firewood • women collect and carry buckets of water at constant risk from mines/in the open/ no protection	5	marker's discretion up to 2/3 marks for understanding of the boys and their environment/car up to 2/3 marks for understanding of local people and their environment
4.	excitement: • '"There! There!"' (line 22) – possible recognition of village disappointment: • 'But nothing distinguishes one village from another' (line 22) – landscape flattened • 'heaps of rubble' (line 23) – indistinguishable compared to how it was nostalgic/wistful: • 'He remembers how he ran around on the paths and fields.' (line 24) – memory of freedom • 'Only the roads are safe.' (line 25) – loss of freedom to run shock: • 'Now the plain is the most mined place in the world.' (lines 24–25) – outrage at devastation	4	two feelings, with quotation and explanation needed each time, for 4 marks

| 5. | 'The ditches are full of wild, dark-red short-stemmed tulips … must be admired at distance. Picking them would be risky.' (lines 27–28) symbolism:
• tulips represent a thing of beauty but cannot be gathered/possessed as in dangerous zone
• nature will always try to survive
• symbol of lives/life lost
• look but do not touch

 '"children sell chains of pink tulips"' (line 30) symbolism:
• exaggerated nostalgia/promotional pre-war literature using colourful flowers

 '"cherries, apricots, almond and pear trees jostle for the attention of the traveller."' (lines 30–31) symbolism:
• exaggerated nostalgia/promotional pre-war literature using an array of trees fighting for prominence

 'they spot a lone rebellious cherry tree or two that have survived bombs' (lines 32–33) symbolism:
• the trees/nature are stubbornly/defiantly determined to survive against all the odds | 6 | quotation, with thoughtful understanding of symbolism, of three plants needed |
| **TOTAL** | | **25** | |

2. *The Idea of Perfection* by Kate Grenville

Level 1

Q		Answer	Mark	Additional guidance
1.	(a)	*'not real flash'* – not sophisticated/not showy/ not expensive looking/not posh	1	1 mark that shows understanding
	(b)	outside: • 'The front gate sagged off a single hinge' (lines 1–2) • 'a length of gutter slanted across the front porch' (line 2) inside: • 'Inside everything was broken, faded, worn-out, improvised' (lines 3–4) • 'a length of white cord hanging out of its sash' (line 4) • 'glass swans…that had been broken and glued together again' (lines 5–6) • 'the taps were covered by a brown-paper bag' (line 6) • 'brown-paper bag with DO NOT USE in big letters.' (lines 6–7)	2	1 mark for each
2.		• worried that she would break the china: 'imagining matching tea-cups that she would chip' (lines 8–9) • worried that she would mark the tables: 'and polished tables that she would scratch' (line 9) • worried that she is like an intruder/ invading privacy/being a stranger in someone's house: 'with the private shape of someone else's feet still in the shoes' (lines 9–10) • not wanting to be so aware of other people's lives/to be reminded that it is someone else's home/to sleep in someone else's old bed: 'the troughs made by other people's lives still in the mattress.' (lines 10–11)	6	up to 2 marks for each reason supported with an appropriate quotation

3.	sentimental: • 'the ornaments had all been broken at least once already' (line 13) – she likes to keep precious things even though they are broken mean: • 'the ornaments had all been broken at least once already' (line 13) – not prepared to spend money on new things lazy: • 'when the kitchen tap … had to be fitted back on' (line 14) – she does not get around to mending things • 'The fridge door, speckled with dust' (line 15) – she does not like to clean likes people/memories: • 'covered with photos of people lined up' (lines 15–16) – enjoys remembering occasions with friends welcoming/friendly: • 'A space had been cleared among the photos for a note' (line 18) – she takes care to make sure the note is seen • *Welcome, make yourself at home.'* (line 18) – takes the trouble to leave a note	**6**	up to 3 marks for each impression, supported with evidence and explanation
4. (a)	• 'There was grass as faded and dry as straw' (line 22) – simile • 'ribbons of bark' (line 24) – metaphor	**2**	1 mark for each technique identified
(b)	• 'There was grass as faded and dry as straw' (line 22) – the grass has lost its colour and has become yellow and dry from lack of water • 'ribbons of bark' (line 24) – the bark is in long, thin strips	**4**	up to 2 marks for each explanation

| 5. | it looks different:
• 'light was beginning to thicken into gold' (line 30) – there is a strange/unusual light
• 'the sky was always there, big and easy-going.' (line 35) – the sky seems unusually vast and unbroken

it makes Harley think differently:
• 'The city became merely a dream' (line 31) – the city, where she usually lives, has become just a distant memory
• 'The city … as distant as something you had read about in a book' (lines 31–32) – the city, where she used to live, seems just to be in her imagination
• 'something you could remember, or not, as you pleased.' (lines 32–33) – the city, where she used to live, is in her imagination which she can dip in and out of
• 'The country made the city and all its anxieties seem small and silly' (line 33) – all her worries that she had in the city have become unimportant in the country
• 'the sun moving through its path was a long slow drama' (lines 34–35) – time seems to move unusually slowly | 4 | answers may refer to the ways it looks and/or the way it makes Harley think

up to 2 marks for each reason with relevant quotation, showing thoughtful understanding |
| **TOTAL** | | **25** | |

2. *The Idea of Perfection* by Kate Grenville

Level 2

Q	Answer	Mark	Additional guidance
1.	outside: rundown/neglected/not showy: • *'not real flash'* (line 1) • 'The front gate sagged off a single hinge' (lines 1–2) • 'a length of gutter slanted across the front porch' (line 2) inside: unsophisticated/not showy/unkempt/ damaged/tired/shabby/poor looking: • *'not real flash'* (line 1) • 'Inside everything was broken, faded, worn-out, improvised' (lines 3–4) • 'a length of white cord hanging out of its sash' (line 4) • 'glass swans … that had been broken and glued together again' (lines 5–6) • 'the taps were covered by a brown-paper bag' (line 6) • 'brown-paper bag with DO NOT USE in big letters.' (lines 6–7)	4	up to 2 marks for each well-supported impression
2.	dread/anxiety/trepidation: • 'Harley had dreaded Lorraine Smart's house' (line 8) – she was anxious about living in someone else's/a stranger's house and what she would find • she thought Lorraine Smart might live up to her name and have a 'smart' house worried: • 'imagining matching tea-cups that she would chip' (lines 8–9) – worried that she might break the china • 'polished tables that she would scratch' (line 9) – worried that she might mark the tables	4	up to 2 marks for each mood with appropriate supporting quotation

	uncomfortable/a disturbance/awkward:		
	• 'the private shape of some else's feet still in the shoes' (lines 9–10) – worried that she is like an intruder/a stranger in someone else's house • 'the troughs made by other people's lives still in the mattress.' (lines 10–11) – not wanting to be so aware of other people's lives/not wanting to be reminded that it is someone else's home relief: • 'But she was starting to feel that she would probably like Lorraine Smart' (line 12) – her attitude is changed • 'She liked the fact that the ornaments had all been broken' (line 13) – felt pleased that precious things were not in good repair/felt at home • 'when the kitchen tap came off in her hand … she felt at home.' (lines 14–15) – relieved that everything was not in perfect order, like her own home relaxed: • 'she felt at home.' (lines 14–15) – she feels comfortable, as if she were in her own home comforted/reassured/cheered: • 'photos of people lined up … smiling.' (lines 15–16) – she likes the fact that Lorraine Smart seems to enjoy her friends/pleased to see smiling faces		
3.	sentimental: • 'the ornaments had all been broken at least once already' (line 13) – she likes to keep precious things even though they are broken miserly/tight-fisted: • 'the ornaments had all been broken at least once already' (line 13) – not prepared to spend money on new things	**6**	marker's discretion up to 2/3 marks for two/three supported impressions, depending on detail

		lazy: • 'when the kitchen tap … had to be fitted back on' (line 14) – she does not get around to mending things • 'The fridge door, speckled with dust,' (lines 14–15) – she does not like to clean likes people/memories: • 'covered with photos of people lined up,' (lines 15–16) – enjoys remembering occasions with friends welcoming/friendly: • 'A space had been cleared among the photos for a note' (line 18) – she takes care to make sure the note is seen • *Welcome, make yourself at home.'* (line 18) – takes the trouble to leave a note		
4.		• 'There was grass as faded and dry as straw' (line 22) – simile – the grass has lost its colour and has become yellow and dry from lack of water/the drought • 'where other shrubs had given up' (line 23) – personification – plants unable to survive • 'gum tree hung with ragged ribbons of bark' (lines 23–24) – metaphor – the bark from the tree is dangling in long thin strips • 'ragged ribbons' (line 24) – alliteration – repeated r sound pulls words together for added effect	4	up to 2 marks for quotation, identification and explanation of each image alliteration is less good as it does not add to image
5.	(a)	the view: • 'The sun was beginning to lower itself down toward the hills' (lines 29–30) – as if the sun is suspended and unreal • 'light was beginning to thicken into gold' (line 30) – there is a strange/unusual light • 'the sky was always there, big and easy-going.' (line 35) – the sky seems unusually vast and unbroken	5	up to 2 marks for description of the physical view with relevant quotations up to 3 marks for explanation of her thoughts with relevant quotations

	thoughts: • 'The city became merely a dream' (line 31) – the city, where she usually lives, has become just a distant memory • 'The city ... as distant as something you had read about in a book' (lines 31–32) – the city seems to be a figment of her imagination • 'something you could remember, or not, as you pleased.' (lines 32–33) – the city is now in her imagination which she can recall at will • 'The country made the city and all its anxieties seem small and silly' (line 33) – all her worries that she had in the city have become unimportant/ trivial in the country • 'the sun moving through its path was a long slow drama' (lines 34–35) – the constancy of nature/time seems to move unusually slowly		
(b)	• she is a city dweller and so the sky may often be obscured by buildings • she is a city dweller and so she may not see the horizon and the whole sky • she has just come out of a haphazard house and she is struck by the contrast of the beauty of the sky/light • she has forgotten about the beauty/ enormity/constancy of the sky	2	up to 2 marks for well-explained and thoughtful response
TOTAL		**25**	

13

3. *Every Good Boy* by David Nicholls

Level 1

Q		Answer	Mark	Additional guidance
1.	(a)	pleased/excited: • 'grinning from behind its immense bulk' (lines 2–3)	2	1 mark for reaction 1 mark for quotation
	(b)	upset/sad/horrified: • 'My mother looked as if she might cry.' (line 5) • '"Take it back, please, I'm begging you."' (line 5)	2	1 mark for reaction 1 mark for one quotation
2.		personification/metaphor: • 'looming oppressively' (line 20) – standing/rising over menacingly/ domineering the space simile: • 'like an angry drunk' (lines 20–21) – large, dominant, formidable simile: • 'The keys were chipped and discoloured like fungal toenails' (line 23) – discoloured/ yellow and uneven metaphor: • 'the keys beyond this were pure percussion, triangle and bass drum.' (lines 25–26) – the notes sound out of tune and with no tone personification: • 'oozed malevolence' (line 26) – seeped/ leaked hatred/evil simile/personification: • 'thrumming along to the TV as if possessed' (line 27) – has an evil mind of its own metaphor: • 'Two treacherous candle-holders sprouted from the black lacquer' (lines 27–28) – dangerous candle-holders which grab at you grow out of the piano	3 + 3	1 mark for naming technique, 1 mark for quotation, 1 mark for explanation, for both choices

		simile: • 'sprouted from the black lacquer like horns' (lines 27–28) – grow from the piano like devilish horns metaphor: • 'snagging my mother's cardies' (line 28) – catching/tearing her cardigan simile/personification: • 'as if the piano might hurl itself at her' (line 30) – the piano might throw/launch itself at her and attack her		
3.	(a)	• 'At the age of nine I was remarkable for being entirely without ability' (line 9) – he feels he has no talent or gift • 'My sister was a gifted and influential majorette' (lines 9–10) – she is good at, and important in, her chosen hobby/it makes him feel inadequate • 'my older brother could dismantle things' (line 10) – his brother has a logical/scientific mind and can do things that he cannot do • 'I could … do nothing well' (line 11) – he feels he is hopeless at everything • 'Graceless, charmless, physically and socially inept' (lines 11–12) – he feels hopeless in every way • 'I lacked even the traditional intelligence of the nerdy.' (lines 12–13) – he feels he does not even have the cleverness of a boring but intelligent person	4	two quotations explained for 4 marks
	(b)	he thinks his son is not very good at anything/untalented: • '"But there must be *something* you can do"' (lines 12–13) • 'my father would sigh as I fumbled the ball' (lines 13–14) • '"Everybody can do *something*."' (line 14)	2	1 mark for sensible thought 1 mark for supporting quotation

15

4.	answers may refer to: • father and Uncle Tony arriving drunk with old piano from the pub • mother's reaction – cross at/irritated by father and Uncle Tony bringing piano home • the narrator's sad honesty at his own inadequacies • the possibility that he thought he could play like Mozart • description of the piano as a monster • the mother thinks there might be a dead body in the piano • sounds of the piano are odd • able to relate to own family experience	4	candidate's own response up to 4 marks for understanding and explanation of humour
5.	answers may refer to: • the mother may get rid of the piano as she did not like it from the start which causes a family argument • the mother or the father could suggest piano lessons for their son and the piano is tuned but he is hopeless at playing it • the mother or the father could suggest piano lessons for their son, the piano is tuned and he does become a brilliant player and begins to feel more confident and equal to his brother and sister • his brother and sister take up the piano and are now brilliant at that as well as other things	5	candidate's own response up to 5 marks for sensible suggestions, to include some family reaction
TOTAL		25	

3. *Every Good Boy* by David Nicholls

Level 2

Q	Answer	Mark	Additional guidance
1.	father: pleased/excited/proud of themselves/ pleased to have something for free: • 'grinning from behind its immense bulk' (lines 2–3) – pleased with their find and ability to bring it home • "'They were going to throw it away so I said we'd have it.'" (lines 3–4)/"'But it's free! It's a completely free piano!'" (line 6) mother: upset/horrified/dismayed: • 'My mother looked as if she might cry.' (line 5) • "'Take it back, please, I'm begging you.'" (line 5) – cannot bear the thought of the piano in the house • does not like the thought of where the piano has come from • shocked at the size and/or look of the piano • "'What are we going to do with a piano, Michael? You can't play it, I can't play it'" (line 7) – realises it is going to be a useless piece of furniture	4	two reactions with quotation and explanation needed for 4 marks
2.	personification/metaphor: • 'looming oppressively' (line 20) – standing/rising over menacingly/domineering the space simile: • 'like an angry drunk' (lines 20–21) – large, dominant, formidable simile: • 'The keys were chipped and discoloured like fungal toenails' (line 23) – discoloured/yellow and uneven	6	three techniques to be quoted, identified and explained

	metaphor: • 'the keys beyond this were pure percussion, triangle and bass drum.' (lines 25–26) – the notes sounded out of tune and with no tone personification : • 'oozed malevolence' (line 26) – seeped/ leaked hatred/evil personification/simile: • 'thrumming along to the TV as if possessed' (line 27) – has an evil mind of its own metaphor: • 'Two treacherous candle-holders sprouted from the black lacquer' (lines 27–28) – dangerous candle-holders grew out of the piano simile: • 'sprouted from the black lacquer like horns' (lines 27–28) – grew devilish horns/ grew horns as if from the devil metaphor: • 'snagging my mother's cardies' (line 28) – catching/tearing her cardigan simile/personification: • 'as if the piano might hurl itself at her' (line 30) – the piano might throw/launch itself at her and attack her		
3.	prim and proper/respectable: • 'handsome semi-detached house' (lines 38–39) – well-kept/good-looking house • 'lace-curtained windows' (line 40) – likes to stay private • 'delicate and precise renditions' (line 40) – she plays the piano quietly and carefully old fashioned: • 'popular classics, hymns, old Noël Coward numbers' (lines 40–41) – enjoys the old and traditional musical: • 'delicate and precise renditions' (line 40) – plays with skill	6	three impressions needed, supported with evidence and explanation

	• 'popular classics, hymns, old Noël Coward numbers' (lines 40–41) – has a varied repertoire longs for past/nostalgic: • 'struggling to conceal her resentment at the new estate' (lines 42–43) – barely hides her annoyance at the new housing and its inhabitants in need of money: • 'polite but sour' (line 42) – does not want the work, but feels she must be polite to get employment • 'Widowed' (line 45) – in need of the income as no husband to support her • 'with a shrinking number of … pupils' (line 45) – income lowered as pupils dwindle • 'could not afford to be a snob' (line 46) – had to work even though she wanted not to		
4.	specific words/quotations of characters: • 'red-faced from exertion and lunchtime pints' (line 3) – come back, puffed out, having had too much to drink/visual picture • 'fumbled the ball' (lines 13–14) – pathetic at catching • 'fell from the tree' (line 14) – cannot even stay in a tree • 'bounced clear of the trampoline' (line 14) – cannot even land on the trampoline • '"I keep thinking there's a corpse in there"' (line 29) – the wooden shape of the piano looks like a coffin/mother's thought of a dead body/mother's death wish to it specific words/quotations that describe the piano: • 'monster' (line 2) – grotesque • 'like an angry drunk' (lines 20–21) – invades your space • 'the keys were chipped and discoloured like fungal toenails.' (line 23) – piano keys revolting/disgusting	**4**	up to 4 marks for two explained examples

	• ""I keep thinking there's a corpse in there"" (line 29) – the piano shape reminds the reader of a coffin • 'to suggest falling snowflakes or dropped saucepans' (lines 31–32) – pretending his awful hacking at keys are compositions the narrator's honest portrayal of himself: • 'At the age of nine I was remarkable for being entirely without ability.' (line 9) – total honesty/endearing • 'I could … do nothing well.' (line 11) – total honesty/endearing/pathos • 'Graceless, charmless, physically and socially inept' (lines 11–12) – the list of inadequacies is comic • 'I lacked even the traditional intelligence of the nerdy.' (lines 12–13) – social awareness/ use of slang vocabulary/ironic humour the comparison of himself to Mozart: • 'Mozart was composing concertos at nine,' (line 15) – outlandish comparison general feelings about the characters/ interactions: • ""But it's *free*! It's a completely free piano!"" (line 6) – trying to be persuasive • ""tearing her own ears off"" (line 37) – realistic/believable family behaviour or relate ideas from passage to own experience		
5.	no: • the mother will be discouraging • the piano is not in tune/the pedals do not work • the narrator is never very good at anything and has no talent for anything • he will not get on with Mrs Chin • Mrs Chin will not want to teach him the music he wants to play, e.g. *Jaws*	5	up to 5 marks for well-reasoned/relevant answers points all in support of piano being a success or points all against the piano being a success or a mixture of the two

	yes: • he wants to be like Mozart • his father and Uncle Tony will be supportive • Mrs Chin will bring out the best in him • Mrs Chin is cheap and local so he will be able to continue lessons		
TOTAL		**25**	

4. *The Winning Mind* by Sebastian Coe

Level 1

Q		Answer	Mark	Additional guidance
1.	(a)	his father	**1**	1 mark
	(b)	it is surprising that he does not expect him to win the race but will be happy if he just gets a medal	**2**	up to 2 marks for understanding why the response is surprising
2.	(a)	• 'With buckets of adrenaline' (line 6) – metaphor • 'his stirring words ringing in my ears' (line 6) – metaphor • 'like free beer' (line 7) – simile	**2**	1 mark for either metaphor 1 mark for simile
	(b)	• he is pumped up ready to race • he is encouraged by his father's/coach's words which are spilling round in his head • he sets off as fast as people rushing to get free beer	**2**	up to 2 marks for understanding of two of the three phrases
3.		joyful: • 'I completed the first lap … faster than anyone had ever done previously' (line 8) – he thinks he is doing so well/running so fast • 'The tactics worked perfectly,' (line 9) – elation/pleased with himself – he thinks he is doing so well/running so fast/winning disappointed: • 'the world began to cave in' (line 10) – huge disappointment/frustration – things not going so well, towards the end of the race/he realises that the dream will not happen • 'I was concerned simply with reaching the finishing line!' (lines 11–12) – resignation/upset – he realises that he cannot win but just needs to finish	**2 + 4**	2 marks for identifying quotations up to 4 marks for explanations
4.	(a)	• never give up during the race/persevere • never give up even though losing may hurt	**3**	up to three lessons needed for 3 marks

		• pace yourself • hard work/training needed • analyse the competition • consider the outcome of a race • focus/plan for the future		
	(b)	• he broke his/a world record • he held 800m records, in total, for eighteen years	**2**	both outcomes needed
5.	(a)	sense of humour: • 'with a mischievous glint in his eye.' (line 4) – has a twinkle in his eye/light-hearted approach to the race • '"And we'll find out what the b******s are made of!"'(lines 4–5) – amusing attitude towards the other competitors • '"That was phenomenal! All you have to do next time is to run the second lap as fast as you did the first!"' (lines 18–19) – gently sarcastic supportive/encouraging: • 'his stirring words ringing in my ears' (line 6) – Coe takes inspiring words into the race • 'I was criticised on every side by everybody – apart from my father' (lines 17–18) – he is behind him even when the going gets tough/everyone else seems against him • 'we both knew that I had much hard work to do' (lines 19–20) – they are in it together down to earth: • '"And we'll find out what the b******s are made of!"'(lines 4–5) – straight talking father's love and understanding: • he knows best how to motivate Coe/he cares deeply/he is teaching life lessons not just sporting lessons	**4**	up to 4 marks for two qualities with explanations candidate may use quotations or answer in own words

	loyalty: • he is always there for Coe/he sticks up for him when others do not/he believes in him tough: • keeps Coe training and improving good teacher: • teaches him never to give up/to learn from failure/to learn from past experiences • if you are used to winning it will be painful when you lose • do not assume that winners do not feel a failure if they lose • once you get used to winning it is even worse when you lose		
(b)		**3**	up to 3 marks for understanding
TOTAL		**25**	

4. *The Winning Mind* by Sebastian Coe

Level 2

Q	Answer	Mark	Additional guidance
1.	• 'With buckets of adrenaline' (line 6) – metaphor – he is pumped up/full of energy • 'his stirring words ringing in my ears' (line 6) – metaphor – his uplifting words were echoing around my head • 'like free beer' (line 7) – simile – he sets off as fast as people rushing to get free beer	4	up to 4 marks for two techniques quoted, identified and explained
2.	elation/pleased with himself: • 'I completed the first lap…faster than anyone had ever done previously' (line 8) – he thinks he is doing so well/running so fast • 'The tactics worked perfectly,' (line 9) – he thinks he is doing so well/running so fast/winning huge disappointment/frustration: • 'the world began to cave in' (line 10) – things not going so well towards the end of the race/he realises that the dream will not happen resignation/realistic: • 'I was concerned simply with reaching the finishing line!' (lines 11–12) – he realises that he cannot win but just needs to finish determined/proud/relief: • 'my doggedness gained me bronze' (line 15) – he does not give up and at least finishes with a medal hurt/upset: • 'The press gave me an absolute slating' (line 17) – upset that the press heavily criticised him • 'I was criticised on every side by everybody' (lines 17–18) – despite running his best and achieving a bronze medal he receives criticism	6	up to 2 marks for each feeling with relevant quotation/evidence and explanation

		amused/thankful/relieved: • "'That was phenomenal! All you have to do next time is to run the second lap as fast as you did the first!'" (lines 18–19) – pleased that his father did not join in the criticism		
3.	• never give up during the race/persevere • never give up even though losing may hurt • pace yourself • hard work/training needed • analyse the competition • consider the outcome of a race • plan for the future • he broke his/a world record • he held 800m records, in total, for eighteen years	5	up to 3 marks for three lessons up to 2 marks for the outcomes
4.	sense of humour: • 'with a mischievous glint in his eye.' (line 4) – has a twinkle in his eye/light-hearted approach to the race • "'And we'll find out what the b******s are made of!'"(lines 4–5) – amusing attitude towards the other competitors • "'That was phenomenal! All you have to do next time is to run the second lap as fast as you did the first!'" (lines 18–19) – gently sarcastic supportive/encouraging: • 'his stirring words ringing in my ears' (line 6) – Coe takes inspiring words into the race • 'I was criticised on every side by everybody – apart from my father' (lines 17–18) – he is behind him even when the going gets tough/everyone else seems against him • 'we both knew that I had much hard work to do' (lines 19–20) – they are in it together	6	three qualities needed supported with quotations and explanations or with overview understanding and explanations

	down to earth: • "'And we'll find out what the b******s are made of!'"(lines 4–5) – straight talking father's love and understanding: • he knows best how to motivate Coe/he cares deeply/he is teaching life lessons not just sporting lessons loyalty: • he is always there for Coe/he sticks up for him when others do not/he believes in him tough: • keeps Coe training and improving good teacher: • teaches him never to give up/to learn from failure/to learn from past experiences		
5.	in sport: • 'Never underestimate the competition' (line 40) – there will be more than one person challenging you/do not concern yourself with only the person/runner who is your nearest rival as someone may come through from the back of the field in business: • 'While you are focusing on challenging your nearest rival ... others are working equally hard.' (lines 41–43) • 'enjoying your position as market leader, others are working equally hard.' (lines 42–43) • 'Never doubt that there is someone else ready to seize the moment and hungry to displace your market dominance.' (lines 43–44) • while you are working hard do not overlook that there are others doing the same/do not think that you will always be ahead or that you can bask in your success/there are others always keen to rival you	**4**	up to 4 marks for two areas of his life explained candidates may use and explain quotations or explain entirely in own words

	in the Olympic bid: • 'it would have been easy to assume that Paris was the biggest threat to London's challenge, but the other cities were equally hungry for success.' (lines 44–46) – although it seemed that Paris was the only rival, other countries stood a chance too and should not be ignored		
TOTAL		**25**	

5. *Travels with Charley* by John Steinbeck

Level 1

Q		Answer	Mark	Additional guidance
1.	(a)	• 'ripped the water like a black sheet' (lines 1–2) • 'It hammered like a fist.' (line 2) • 'The whole top of an oak tree crashed down' (line 2) • 'grazing the cottage where we watched.' (lines 2–3) • 'The next gust stove one of the big windows in.' (line 3) • 'Electric power and telephone lines went out with the first blast,' (lines 4–5)	2	two quotations needed for 2 marks
	(b)	• the trees behave as if they are flimsy grasses blown over by the force of the wind • boats career/slide quickly up and onto the beach • waves crash into the upper floors of houses • the rising water goes right over the pier	2	two effects, in own words, needed for 2 marks
2.		simile: • 'ripped the water like a black sheet.' (line 1–2) – the wind is so powerful that it tears the sea as if it is a bit of dark material • 'It hammered like a fist.' (line 2) – the wind is punching down with clenched/ angry fists on the land/water • 'the wind rip at earth and sea like a surging pack of terriers.' (line 6) – the wind is behaving like angry/chasing/hunting dogs ready for the kill • 'The trees plunged and bent like grasses' (line 7) – the wind is so strong that the trees are flung around as if they are very flimsy and light	2+2+2	well-chosen example, and explanation of each technique (simile, metaphor and onomatopoeia) needed for 6 marks

		• 'swinging like a weathervane away from the changing wind.' (lines 12–13) – the wind is so strong and wild that it is forcing the boat to change direction metaphor: • 'The wind ... ripped the water' (line 1) – the wind is so strong that it seems to tear the water apart • 'whipped water' (line 7) – the water is thrown around/churned like cream thickening • 'raised a cream of foam' (line 7) – the water is thrown around and seems to thicken like cream • 'A boat ... tobogganed up on the shore' (line 8) – slides up the beach quickly/ out of control as if sliding on snow/ice onomatopoeia: • 'hammered' (line 2) – harsh sound of wind emphasised • 'crashed' (line 2) – enables reader to hear the sudden/harsh sound of the oak falling to the ground • 'rip' (line 6) – short, quick tearing sound • 'plunged' (line 7) – slow long sound to emphasise the noise of the falling trees • 'whipped' (line 7) – short snappy sound to emphasise the effect of the wind on the water		
3.	(a)	Charley dog: • 'he found a warm place under a table and went to sleep' (lines 18–19) narrator: • 'I found myself running, fighting the wind' (line 31)	2	1 mark for each quotation
	(b)	• Charley dog is not nervous/he is completely unaware of the storm/he is used to hurricanes and bad weather • the narrator wants to save his boat/he is panicking/he is aware of the dangers	2	1 mark for each sensible suggestion

30

4.	(a)	• personification • the boat is reluctant to move in the wind and puts up a fight and seems to cry in pain/despair/revolt	**1** **2**	1 mark up to 2 marks for explanation of picture
	(b)	to show us how much he cares about the boat, almost as if it is a person	**2**	up to 2 marks for understanding
5.		stage one: • violent/wild/fierce/forceful/powerful – the wind is strong and causing widespread damage on the land stage two: • calm/still/silent/eerie – the wind drops in the eye of the storm, making it suddenly quiet and calm, therefore unnerving stage three: • relentless/vicious/surprising/shocking/ damaging/buffeting – the wind has suddenly returned, blowing in the opposite direction/from the other side causing greater damage	**6**	up to 2 marks for each relevant word choice and supporting explanation
TOTAL			**25**	

5. *Travels with Charley* by John Steinbeck

Level 2

Q	Answer	Mark	Additional guidance
1.	• 'The wind … ripped the water' (line 1) – metaphor – the wind is so violent that it seems to tear the water apart • 'ripped the water like a black sheet.' (lines 1–2) – simile – the wind is so powerful that it tears the sea as if it is a bit of dark material • 'It hammered like a fist.' (line 2) – simile – the wind is punching down with clenched/angry fists on the land/water • 'the wind rip at earth and sea like a surging pack of terriers.' (line 6) – simile – the wind is behaving like angry/chasing/hunting dogs ready for the kill • 'The trees plunged and bent like grasses' (line 7) – simile – the wind is so forceful that the trees are flung around as if they are very flimsy and light • 'the whipped water raised a cream of foam' (line 8) – metaphor – the water is thrown around and seems to thicken like cream • 'A boat … tobogganed up the shore' (lines 7–8) – metaphor – slides up the beach quickly/out of control as if sliding on snow/ice • 'swinging like a weathervane away from the changing wind.' (lines 12–13) – simile – the wind is so powerful and wild that it is forcing the boat to change direction	6	up to 6 marks for three well-chosen quotations with identification and explanation
2.	Charley dog: • 'he found a warm place under a table and went to sleep' (lines 18–19) – Charley dog is not nervous/he is completely unaware of the storm/he is completely inactive/he is unable to foresee the danger/he is used to bad weather/he has always survived	4	up to 2 marks each for quotation and explanation which describe the dog's and the narrator's reactions

	narrator: • 'I found myself running, fighting the wind' (line 31) – he is scared/foresees danger/ takes action to save his boat/he is panicking and not thinking clearly/he is aware of the dangers		
3.	'dragged fighting' (line 28), 'protesting' (line 28), 'crying' (line 29), 'cried' (line 35), 'whined' (line 36), 'plunged' (line 36), 'like a frightened calf' (line 36) • his choices of words and use of emotive vocabulary show his empathy for its situation • he thinks of the *Fayre Eleyne* as if it is a person • he transfers human emotions to it/some candidates may refer to personification	4	up to 4 marks for two vocabulary choices quoted and explained
4.	he has saved the *Fayre Eleyne* writer: • he feels proud that he has secured her safety and her anchor is still in place • he feels heroic to have overcome the storm and his ordeal • he feels triumphant that he has saved his precious boat • he is surprised he has the knife he needed to do the job and that he was successful wife: • she might feel angry that his actions put him at risk/may lose his life for the boat • she might feel angry that he didn't stop when she asked him to • she might feel jealous/upset as his actions show he thinks more of the boat than her	5	1 mark up to 2 marks for a well-explained feeling up to 2 marks for a well-explained feeling

5.	quotations must show evidence of understanding nature of storm at each stage	6	up to 2 marks for each best/relevant quotation choice with supporting explanation
	stage one/the beginning:		
	• 'The wind struck' (line 1)		
	• 'It hammered like a fist.' (line 2)		
	• 'We watched the wind rip at earth and sea' (line 6)		
	• 'The trees plunged and bent like grasses' (line 7)		
	• 'Houses … took waves in their second-storey windows' (lines 8–9)		
	• 'But the rising tide washed over my high pier.' (lines 10–11)		
	explanation for any will include:		
	• violent/wild/fierce/forceful/powerful		
	• the wind is strong and causing widespread damage on the land		
	stage two/the eye:		
	• 'The wind stopped as suddenly as it had begun' (line 20)		
	• 'The silence was like a rushing sound.' (line 23)		
	• 'we were in the eye of Donna' (lines 23–24)		
	• 'the still and frightening calm in the middle of the revolving storm.' (line 24)		
	explanation for any will include:		
	• calm/still/silent/eerie		
	• the wind drops in the eye of the storm, making it suddenly quiet and calm, therefore unnerving		
	stage three/the continuation:		
	• 'And then the other side struck us, the wind from the opposite direction.' (lines 25–26)		
	explanation might include:		
	• relentless/vicious/surprising/shocking/damaging/buffeting		
	• the wind has suddenly returned, blowing in the opposite direction/from the other side causing greater damage		
TOTAL		**25**	

6. *Brazil* by Michael Palin

Level 1

Q		Answer	Mark	Additional guidance
1.	(a)	• the dogs race/run to the plane • they bark noisily • they caper/frolic around	**2**	up to 2 marks for two actions
		• they sense the arrival of an 'interloper' or stranger • they hear the sound of the engine	**1**	1 mark for one reason
	(b)	• the people appear at the doors quietly	**2**	1 mark for people's reaction one reason needed for 1 mark
		• the people are used to planes arriving • the people are expecting him		
2.	(a)	• 'make an entrance of self-conscious swagger.' (lines 16–17) – they want to make an impression/feel confident but they are also feeling wary/apprehensive	**1 + 2**	1 mark for one quotation up to 2 marks for understanding men's reactions
		• 'the men gather around appraising us curiously.' (line 19) – they are curious/inquisitive so they group around watching with interest		
	(b)	• they are keeping out of the sun • they are disinterested • they are not expected to join in with the men	**1**	reward any similar or sensible suggestion
	(c)	• they play a joke on him/set him up: the laughter is because they know that he is about to fail/they know that he will not be as good as they are	**2**	up to 2 marks, depending on detail of response and level of understanding
		• to show off how good they are with the bow and arrow/it gives them a bit of power over a sophisticated visitor	**1**	1 mark for understanding

3.	(a)	he expects them to be unafraid as they are usually aggressive fighters	2	'fearless' and 'ferocious' to be explained in own words
	(b)	they do not fight him, but are friendly: • a man asks for his pen and writes in his book fluently/with ease • another man takes his hat and cheerily puts it on his head/seems to enjoy the joke	4	up to 2 marks for each example, which includes understanding of friendliness of actions
4.		• 'Aeroplanes are the lifeline to the outside world.' (line 6–7) – metaphor • he means that they are isolated/cut off and have to be self-reliant, until there is an emergency, when they may need to use the aeroplane link to save lives	3	1 mark for identifying technique up to 2 marks for understanding metaphor in context
5.		through facts: • 'The Yanomami are one of 200 or so indigenous tribes' (lines 28–29) • 'There were estimated to be some five million Indians in Brazil' (line 30) through description: • 'bumpy grass runway' (line 2) • 'There are no roads that lead here, or even a navigable river.' (line 6) • 'curious little boys in long red shorts' (line 12) explains way of life: • 'any arrival from the sky is greeted with expectation.' (lines 5–6) • 'They carry bows and very long bamboo arrows' (line 17)	4	reward two acceptable features of travel writing/genre, each supported with quotation/evidence
TOTAL			25	

6. *Brazil* by Michael Palin

Level 2

Q		Answer	Mark	Additional guidance
1.		• the dogs race/scamper to the plane, barking madly • they hear the sound of the aeroplane engine because of their acute hearing • they sense the arrival of an 'interloper' or stranger/they are curious	**2**	one reason needed for 1 mark 1 mark for explanation
2.	(a)	boys: • 'curious little boys' (line 12) – the boys are interested/inquisitive but know that it is for the men to greet the visitor women and girls: • 'They're followed, a little more warily, by young girls and, with them, older women' (lines 14–15) – the girls and women are more nervous/cautious and they know that it is the men's role to greet the visitor	**2**	up to 2 marks for explaining quotations 'curious' and 'warily' or in own words
	(b)	• 'self-conscious swagger' (line 17) – they want to appear assertive/in control at arrival of newcomer but are not used to outsiders/visitors and so are uncertain; they give a show of confidence but seem ill at ease in presence of newcomer • 'the men gather around appraising us curiously.' (line 19) – they group themselves with solidarity and watch the newcomers inquisitively to assess the situation • 'one of them … and sends an arrow flying high into the air.' (line 20) – he shows off his skill with a bow and arrow knowing that Palin will not be able to outshine him so he will have the advantage • 'Then he gives me his bow and bids me do the same.' (lines 20–21) – he is polite but he knows that Palin will not be able to outshine him so he will have the advantage	**4**	up to 4 marks for two well-selected quotations, with explanations that prove understanding of behaviour towards Palin

	• 'Amid much chortling' (line 21) – they are all waiting for, and enjoying the joke of, Palin's failure to flight/shoot the arrow		
3.	he expects them to be unafraid as traditionally they have been aggressive fighters they do not fight him but are friendly: • a man hands him his bow – his primary weapon of attack – he is offering his weapon in an act of friendliness • a man asks for his pen and writes in his book fluently/with ease • another man takes his hat and cheerily puts it on his head/seems to enjoy the joke	5	1 mark for explanation of 'fearless' and 'ferocious' in own words up to 2 marks for each understanding of friendliness/sophistication of actions
4.	• 'sunlight filtering through the foliage' (line 37) – alliteration – soft 'f' sound emphasises dreamy, hazy quality of what they are seeing • 'a great quiet, broken only by low voices' (lines 37–38) – metaphor – huge silence shattered by their voices and bird sounds which suggest that jungle is a vast place of silence • 'the occasional screech of a bird' (line 38) – onomatopoeia – harsh sound of bird's call which brings sounds of jungle to life • 'similar in dimension to a small football stadium' (lines 39–40) – comparison – enables reader to picture the size of the maloca easily • 'seems to melt into the surrounding forest.' (lines 40–41) – metaphor – it blends in with the forest/seems to disappear into the forest, despite its size • 'Rising protectively behind it' (line 41) – personification – it is as if the granite outcrop is looking over the maloca and guarding it	6	up to 2/3 marks for quotation, identification of technique/feature and explanation two examples needed in more detail or three examples needed in less detail

5.	through facts:	6	best candidates will give three explained examples which indicate an understanding of the genre
	• 'The Yanomami are one of 200 or so indigenous tribes' (lines 28–29)		
	• 'There were estimated to be some five million Indians in Brazil' (line 30)		
	through setting description:		
	• 'bumpy grass runway' (line 2)		
	• 'There are no roads that lead here, or even a navigable river.' (line 6)		
	• 'sunlight filtering through the foliage' (line 37)		
	• 'the maloca appears abruptly' (lines 38–39)		
	• 'construction ... similar in dimension to a small football stadium' (lines 39–40)		
	• 'smooth grey bulk of a granite outcrop, fringed with scrub' (lines 41–42)		
	through description of people:		
	• 'curious little boys in long red shorts' (line 12)		
	• 'women, most of whom wear nothing but a brief decorated red apron' (lines 15–16)		
	• 'As the women stand and watch' (line 18)		
	explains way of life:		
	• 'any arrival from the sky is greeted with expectation.' (lines 5–6)		
	• 'They carry bows and very long bamboo arrows' (line 17)		
	contrast of old and new:		
	• 'Aeroplanes are the lifeline to the outside world.' (lines 6–7)		
	• 'We leave the modern world behind' (lines 35–36)		
	detail/cameos:		
	• 'roused to a frenzy of barking and capering' (lines 2–3)		
	• 'black hair, dark eyes and light brown skin' (lines 12–13)		
	• 'As the women stand and watch' (line 18)		
	• 'Another likes my straw hat' (line 25)		
	• 'as unselfconsciously as an MCC member' (lines 25–26)		
TOTAL		**25**	

7. *The Finest Story in the World* by Rudyard Kipling

Level 1

Q		Answer	Mark	Additional guidance
1.	(a)	• only son • mother a widow • lives in north London • works in a bank • twenty years old	2	up to 2 marks for four facts
	(b)	• 'He would call on me sometimes in the evening instead of running about London with his fellow-clerks' (lines 8–9) – he chooses to visit the narrator instead of going out with work friends • 'and before long … he told me of his aspirations' (lines 9–10) – he confides in the narrator about his hopes	2	1 mark for quotation 1 mark for reasoning
2.	(a)	• metaphor • eyes really lighting up, as if on fire, because he is so excited	1 + 2	1 mark for naming metaphor up to 2 marks for explanation
	(b)	he wants to write his story/he has a good idea for a story	1	1 mark for one sensible reason
3.	(a)	• 'he hardly thanked me' (line 19) – he forgets his thanks as he is so eager to start writing • 'plunged into the work at once' (lines 19–20) – rushes to his writing straight away • 'scratched without stopping' (line 20) – continues to write without taking a break	2	up to 2 marks for appropriate quotation with explanation
	(b)	• 'Charlie sighed' (lines 20–21) – a sign of disappointment • 'tugged his hair' (line 21) – something he does in frustration as thoughts do not come	4	up to 2 marks for each appropriate quotation with explanation

	• 'scratching grew slower' (line 21) – his enthusiastic start begins to become less hurried • 'more erasures' (line 21) – more mistakes and rubbing out • 'The finest story in the world would not come forth.' (line 22) – he cannot put his wonderful story idea into words on paper			
4.	*answers may refer to:* Charlie: • "'It's such a notion!'" (line 18) – enthusiastic but naive • "'It looks such awful rot now'" (line 23) – honest, but does not realise how good the idea is • "'What do you think of it?'" (line 36) – trusting and open with ideas narrator: • "'What's the trouble?'" (line 16) – appears to be taking a kindly interest but is a liar, just leading Charlie along • 'I could not dishearten him by saying the truth' (line 25) – dishonest • "'It needs compression'" (line 31) – dishonest • 'It would be folly to allow his idea to remain in his own inept hands, when I could do so much with it.' (lines 38–39) – thief/unkind as he wants to steal Charlie's idea	4	1 mark for each characteristic and supporting quotation i.e. Charlie's trusting nature/naivety/narrator's ruthlessness 1 mark each for explanation/reasoning	
5. (a)	*answers may refer to:* Charlie: • sad/lonely: until he meets narrator • unworldly: does not call the marker by his proper name • nervous: in the billiard saloon • does not stand up to narrator: when Charlie does not pay for a game/drink • not wanted: the narrator tells him to go home to his mother	2	up to 2 marks for well-reasoned answer	

		or narrator: • must have few friends: spends his time in a public billiard saloon • feel sorry for him: gets stuck with Charlie who is a bore		
	(b)	*answers may refer to:* Charlie: yes: • still feel sorry for Charlie as the narrator will steal his story idea no: • he is much more talented/imaginative than the narrator • he is a nicer person than the narrator or narrator: • no: the narrator is not just lonely, but unkind too • or other reasonable suggestion	2	up to 2 marks for well-reasoned answer
	(c)	*answers may refer to:* Charlie: • he gets a best-selling book with/without narrator's help • he realises narrator's motives, writes his book, gets a better job, becomes successful or narrator: • his conscience gets the better of him • he helps Charlie • Charlie's book is a success • he is the unsung hero/becomes a nice man	3	up to 3 marks for well-reasoned/detailed explanation, supported by ideas from the text
TOTAL			**25**	

7. *The Finest Story in the World* by Rudyard Kipling

Level 2

Q		Answer	Mark	Additional guidance
1.	(a)	• only son • mother a widow • lives in north London • works in a bank • twenty years old	2	up to 2 marks for four facts
	(b)	• wants to achieve something • he wants to write a wonderful story	2	1 mark for understanding of quotation 1 mark for what his aspiration is
2.		• repetition: 'notion' (lines 17 and 18) – emphasis of good idea • imperative verb: 'Do let' (line 18) – persuasive/direct • emotive vocabulary: 'splendid' (line 17), 'ever written' (line 17) – appealing/ engaging • alliteration: 'splendid story' (line 17) – emphasises those words	4	up to 4 marks for identification and explanation of two devices
3.		*answers may refer to:* excited or similar: • 'his eyes flaming with excitement' (lines 12–13) – eyes alight with enthusiasm • '"I've a notion ... splendid story"' (line 17) – wants to get started on his great idea • 'he hardly thanked me' (line 19) – he forgot his thanks as he is so eager to start writing • 'plunged into the work at once' (lines 19–20) – rushes to his writing straight away • 'scratched without stopping' (line 20) – continues to write without taking a break	6	up to 6 marks for two moods explained in detail or more moods explained in less detail two contrasting moods must be mentioned to gain full marks

	disheartened/or similar: • 'Charlie sighed' (lines 20–21) – a sign of disappointment • 'tugged his hair' (line 21) – something he does in frustration as thoughts do not come • 'scratching grew slower' (line 21) – his enthusiastic start becomes to become less hurried as confidence is lowered • 'more erasures' (line 21) – more mistakes and rubbing out • 'The finest story in the world would not come forth.' (line 22) – he cannot put his wonderful story idea into words on paper • '"It looks such awful rot now," he said, mournfully' (line 23) – thinks his story is not as good as he expected proud/or similar: • 'expecting a little approval' (line 29) – is pleased with his efforts • 'for he was proud of those sentences' (lines 29–30) – is pleased with his efforts		
4.	*answers may refer to:* Charlie: • '"It's such a notion!"' (line 18) – enthusiastic but naive • '"It looks such awful rot now"' (line 23) – honest, but does not realise how good the idea is • '"What do you think of it?"' (line 36) – trusting and open with ideas narrator: • '"What's the trouble?"' (line 16) – appears to be taking a kindly interest but is a liar, just leading Charlie along • 'I could not dishearten him by saying the truth' (line 25) – dishonest • '"It needs compression"' (line 31) – dishonest	6	up to 3 marks for each example of dialogue or thought, which accurately depicts that character, with reasoned explanation i.e. Charlie's trusting nature/naivety or narrator's ruthlessness

		• 'it would be folly to allow his idea to remain in his own inept hands, when I could do so much with it.' (lines 44–45) – thief/unkind/ruthless as he wants to steal Charlie's idea		
5.	(a)	*answers may refer to:* feelings towards Charlie: • feel sorry for him – he is sad and lonely and meets narrator who takes advantage of his naive nature and wants to steal his story idea • irritated – he is needy, possibly an unwanted friend feelings towards narrator: • dislike – he is unkind/dishonest and wants to take advantage of Charlie's good story idea and honest nature • sympathetic – possibly Charlie is too needy	4	up to 2 marks for well-reasoned answer about each character
	(b)	personal response	1	1 mark for whom sympathies lie with and short explanation, referring to previous reasons
TOTAL			**25**	

8. *White Fang* by Jack London

Level 1

Q		Answer	Mark	Additional guidance
1.	(a)	• to warn Bill • not to frighten the animal or scare it off • so as not to be heard by the animal	2	two reasons needed for 2 marks
	(b)	turns, looks, stops the dogs	1	stopping the dogs is the main action needed for 1 mark
	(c)	• the wolf would kill their dogs or them • would not be able to continue/get home • the wolf might kill one or both of them • the wolf is not frightened of them	3	answers should refer to killing of dogs/the men in greater detail, or more points in less detail
2.	(a)	• 'trotted' (line 3) – positive/confident • 'slinking form' (line 4) – furtive/secretive • 'trotted with a peculiar, sliding, effortless gait' (lines 4–5) – relaxed/not worried • 'When they halted, it halted' (line 5) – wary/cautious	2	1 mark for quotation and 1 mark for sensible mood
	(b)	• 'Its nose was to the trail' (line 4) – keeping its nose to the ground to pick up the scent of the men • 'regarding them steadily with nostrils that twitched as it caught and studied the scent of them' (lines 5–6) – nose taking in their smell	2	1 mark for quotation or relevant part of quotation 1 mark for explanation
3.	(a)	• 'as cruel as its own fangs' • 'as merciless as the frost itself'	2	1 mark for each
	(b)	• 'as cruel as its own fangs' – cruel in a sharp way that will pierce right through, like the hunger • 'as merciless as the frost itself' – its hunger completely takes over and will not go away/calculating coldly	2	one simile to be explained

4.	answers may include:	4	two points needed with explanations for 4 marks
	• supportive: communicate when in danger		
	• know each other well: joke with each other		
	• keep each other's morale up: joke with each other		
	• easy-going: easy conversation between them		
5. (a)	answers may include:	3	1 mark per advantage (based on text)
	• familiar with terrain		
	• not afraid		
	• past success as killed dogs		
	• strong		
	• better senses		
	• faster		
(b)	candidate's own response	4	answer should reflect understanding of situation and show thoughtfulness
	wolf:		
	• the men may be armed		
	• acting on instinct in own territory		
	• men invading its territory		
	• needs meat to survive		
	dogs:		
	• obedient victims		
	• easy prey for wolf		
	• harnessed in so cannot escape		
	Henry and Bill:		
	• trying to survive		
	• have lost three dogs		
	• anxious because of what has already happened		
	• in difficult conditions and terrain		
TOTAL		**25**	

8. *White Fang* by Jack London

Level 2

Q		Answer	Mark	Additional guidance
1.		Henry whistles • to warn Bill • so as not to frighten the animal or scare it off Bill turns, looks and quietly stops the dogs • to acknowledge Henry's whistle • to assess situation for himself	3	up to 3 marks for men's reactions and reasons
2.	(a)	*answers may refer to the use of:* verbs to describe movement: • 'trotted a furry, slinking form' (lines 3–4) – confident and surreptitious way of moving • 'it trotted with a peculiar, sliding, effortless gait.' (lines 4–5) – confident, moves with ease in own habitat • 'When they halted, it halted' (line 5) – wolf seems to be playing a wary game • 'throwing up its head' (line 5) – using all its senses against the men strong vocabulary: • 'trotted a furry, slinking form' (lines 3–4) – confident and surreptitious way of moving • 'it trotted with a peculiar, sliding, effortless gait.' (lines 4–5) – confident, moves with ease in own habitat • 'throwing up its head' (line 5) – using all its senses against the men • 'regarding them steadily' (line 5–6) – as if in game and unafraid • 'nostrils that twitched as it caught and studied the scent of them' (line 6) – using all its senses against the men reference to the sense of smell: • 'Its nose was to the trail' (line 4) – using sense of smell against the men	4	reward sensible suggestions two quotations needed with two explanations

48

	• 'nostrils that twitched as it caught and studied the scent of them' (line 6) – using sense of smell against the men other language features: • repetition: 'When they halted, it halted' (line 5) – wolf seems to be playing a wary game • metaphors: 'nostrils that twitched as it caught and studied the scent of them' (line 6) – image of wolf using heightened sense of smell against the men		
(b)	• 'as cruel as its own fangs' (line 15) • 'as merciless as the frost itself' (lines 15–16) • 'as cruel as its own fangs' – cruel in a sharp way that will pierce right through, like the hunger • 'as merciless as the frost itself' – its hunger completely takes over and will not go away/calculating coldly	**3**	1 mark for both similes up to 2 marks for explanation of one
3.	*answer could include* • supportive of each other: unspoken communication when wolf first noticed (lines 1–2) – this shows that there is no need for words between them • know each other well: "'Ain't a bit scairt of you," Henry laughed' (line 30) – they know what makes the other laugh • joke with each other/keep each other's morale up: "'Hello, you husky!'" (line 29) – lightens the mood • easy-going with each other: easy conversation between them – shows familiarity • Bill the more dominant: he suggests they try and shoot it – he makes decisions (line 37) • Bill more proactive: he calls to the wolf (line 29), he invites it over (line 29), he waves at it threateningly (line 31), he shouts at it (line 31) – all show that it is Bill, not Henry, who acts quickly	**6**	up to 6 marks three impressions with explanations, using quotations or own words, in less detail or two impressions, using quotations or own words, in more detail

4.		answers may include: • that he is in awe of the wolf • that it is a narrow escape for them • that he is almost glad they hadn't killed it • that he wishes they had killed it • that he is scared of what it might do next • that he is amazed that it seems to sense that it is about to be shot	2	two ideas needed for 2 marks
5.	(a)	answers may include: wolf: • familiar with terrain • not afraid • past success as killed dogs • strong • keener senses • faster men: • the men have a gun which can kill it • the men have a better brain to outwit the wolf • the men want revenge	4	reward at least two sensible suggestions supported by evidence
	(b)	answers may refer to: wolf: • the men are armed • just acting on instinct in own territory • men invading its territory • needs meat to survive dogs: • obedient victims • easy prey for wolf • harnessed in so cannot escape Henry and Bill: • trying to survive • have lost three dogs • anxious because of what has already happened • in difficult conditions and terrain	3	candidate's personal response answer should reflect understanding of men's and animals' situations, and provide support for choice
TOTAL			**25**	

9. *Great Expectations* by Charles Dickens

Level 1

Q		Answer	Mark	Additional guidance
1.	(a)	• damp • misty • frosty • or similar suggestion	**2**	two words for 2 marks
	(b)	• the outside of the window • hedges • grass • rail • gate • signpost	**2**	2 marks for two places either in own words or quotation
2.	(a)	• 'like a coarser sort of spiders' webs' (line 4) – describes the delicate woven shape of the damp on the twigs and grass	**2**	1 mark for finding simile 1 mark for explanation of similie
	(b)	• he cannot see the signpost to the village until he is right up to it	**1**	1 mark for explanation
3.	(a)	• he has stolen a pork pie from the kitchen • he is about to meet the runaway prisoner • he is scared of being caught • he is scared of someone seeing him	**2**	2 marks for two correct suggestions
	(b)	• '"Halloa, young thief!"' (line 15) • 'awakened conscience' (line 16) • 'fixed me so obstinately' (line 16) • 'accusatory manner' (line 17) • 'blubbered' (line 18) • '"I couldn't help it, sir!"' (line 18)	**2**	two phrases for 2 marks
4. (a)		• he thinks the man is asleep and wants to be gentle • he wants to give him a surprise for breakfast • he is unsure of himself • he is possibly quite scared	**2**	two reasons necessary for 2 marks

	(b)	• had been asleep • is not expecting anyone to disturb him • man is wary as he is on the run • man is guilty	**2**	two reasons necessary for 2 marks
	(c)	• has his back to him • looks similar to the man/prisoner he had met previously	**1**	one reason necessary for 1 mark
5.	(a)	*answers could include or be similar to:* • observant: 'It was a rimy morning, and very damp' (line 1) – notices things • sensitive/aware of surroundings: 'I had seen the damp lying on the outside of my little window' (lines 1–2) – notices small detail • sensitive/aware of people: 'it was not the same man, but another man' (line 30) – notices small detail • strong sense of conscience: 'This was very disagreeable to a guilty mind.' (lines 11–12) – knows he has done wrong • imaginative: 'something of a clerical air' (line 16) – thinks animals know his guilty secret • determined: 'had to try back along the river-side' (line 22) – battles his way through mist • honourable: 'who has asked him to get some food' (introduction) – keeping to the agreement • dishonourable: 'Pip has stolen a pork pie' (introduction) – stole the pie • scared: 'everything seemed to run at me' (line 11) – frightened by animals and mist • brave: to steal and meet prisoner • stupid: he could have come to harm	**6**	relevant character word, evidence and explanation needed each time

(b)	*answers may refer to:* feel sorry for him: • young boy out on his own, in the mist • worried about his theft • worried about meeting the prisoner • only a pork pie – nothing more valuable • trying to help someone else • his theft is of something small in value do not feel sorry for him: • should not have stolen • should not have been out on his own • should not have got involved with prisoner • brought it on himself	3	candidate's personal response answer should reflect understanding of situation
TOTAL		**25**	

9. Great Expectations by Charles Dickens

Level 2

Q	Answer	Mark	Additional guidance
1. (a)	• damp • misty • frosty • similar suggestion	2	at least two words/phrases for 2 marks
(b)	• on the outside of the window • hedges • grass • rail • gate • signpost	2	2 marks for two places either in own words or quotation
2.	• 'as if some goblin had been crying there all night, and using the window for a pocket-handkerchief.' (lines 2–3) – like a little sad creature using the window as his handkerchief • 'like a coarser sort of spiders' webs' (line 4) – describes the delicate woven shape of the damp on the twigs and grass • 'like a phantom' (lines 8–9) – as if a ghostly figure is in control of him and directing him	4	1 mark for quoting each simile 1 mark for explanation each time
3.	*answers may refer to:* • 'everything seemed to run at me' (line 11) – things moving towards him/ size emphasised • 'bursting at me through the mist' (line 12) – rushing up at him suddenly/size emphasised • '"A boy with Somebody's else's pork pie!"' (line 13) – animals speaking to him in his imagination • '"Halloa, young thief!"' (line 15) – animals speaking to him in his imagination • 'awakened conscience' (line 16) – newly felt guilt • 'fixed me so obstinately' (line 16) – animals reading his mind in his imagination	4	two explained quotations needed for 4 marks

		• 'accusatory manner' (line 17) – animals reading his mind in his imagination • "'I couldn't help it, sir!'" (line 18) – talking to animals as if they were judging him		
4.		*answers may refer to:* • hopeful/pleased: 'I thought he would be more glad' (line 28) – he thinks he will get a better reception • surprised/confused/shocked: 'not the same man, but another man!' (line 30) – it is not the man he was expecting • frightened/scared: 'he swore an oath at me, made a hit at me' (lines 34–35) – the man nearly hit him • relieved/thankful/pleased: 'he ran into the mist' (line 36) – the man stumbles off	6	up to 6 marks for three appropriate feelings, with explanation using quotations or own words, in less detail or two feelings using quotations or own words, in more detail
5.	(a)	*answers may refer to:* • observant: 'It was a rimy morning, and very damp' (line 1) – notices things • sensitive/aware of surroundings: 'I had seen the damp lying on the outside of my little window' (lines 1–2) – notices small detail • sensitive/aware of people: 'it was not the same man, but another man' (line 30) – notices small detail • strong sense of conscience: 'This was very disagreeable to a guilty mind.' (lines 11–12) – knows he has done wrong • imaginative: 'something of a clerical air' (line 16) – thinks animals know his guilty secret • determined: 'had to try back along the river-side' (line 22) – battles his way through mist • honourable: 'who has asked him to get some food' (introduction) – keeping to the agreement • dishonourable: 'Pip has stolen a pork pie' (introduction) – stole the pie	4	accept any sensible response two characteristics needed for each one: 1 mark for characteristic and supporting quotation/evidence, 1 mark for reasoning

(b)	• scared: 'everything seemed to run at me' (line 11) – frightened by animals and mist • brave: to steal and meet prisoner • stupid: he could have come to harm • feel sorry for him: is an unwilling participant • feel he is foolish – should not have got himself into that situation in the first place • feel worried for him as not sure how it is going to work out, meeting a prisoner in the mist	3		candidate's personal response accept any reasonable response answer should reflect understanding of situation
TOTAL		25		

10. *The History Boys* by Alan Bennett

Level 1

Q	Answer	Mark	Additional guidance
1.	• she is curious/nosy • to know how her pupils are getting on with the new teacher	3	1 mark for curious/nosy up to 2 marks for understanding reasons behind curiosity: her pupils/new teacher
2.	Mrs Lintott/battery chickens: • 'You've force-fed us the facts' (line 12) – lessons driven by learning facts, without discussion, with no freedom Mr Irwin/free-range: • 'we're in the process of running around acquiring flavour.' (lines 12–13) – discussion/thinking time/freedom allowed to become more rounded students	4	up to 2 marks each for two quotations with explanations
3.	polite/agreeable/friendly: • stops him to ask a friendly question about his new teacher: 'How are you all getting on with Mr Irwin?' (line 3) • interested in his answer: 'That's nice to hear.' (line 6) rigid/direct teacher: • teaches using facts/explains things methodically/no freedom within lessons: 'Point A. Point B. Point C.' (line 7) predictable: • teaches in an old-fashioned manner • shocked by/not understanding new teaching methods/ideas • responds as Rudge expects her to self-doubting: • she wonders if she is teaching in the right way/using the right materials pitiful/wistful: • she is sad to think they are having fun in lessons without her: 'Dear me. What fun you must all have.' (line 34)	6	up to 6 marks for two or three impressions depending on detail to include own thoughtful ideas from text or supporting quotations

		inquisitive: • she wants to know what is going on in the lessons: 'How are you getting on with Mr Irwin?' (line 3)		
4.		• 'It makes me grateful for your lessons.' (lines 4–5) – by the end of the text we realise he does not mean that, he is only saying what he knows she wants to hear • 'It's only a metaphor, miss.' (line 10) – he is showing off his knowledge to her to please her • 'I'm just going home now to watch some videos of the *Carry On* films.' (lines 17–18) – he knows this will be annoying to her • 'You never know with him.' (line 22) – deliberately being vague • '(*he is reading from his notes*)' (lines 24–25) – showing off the very different/pompous teaching he is receiving from Mr Irwin • 'Mr Irwin said' (line 20), 'Mr Irwin says' (line 24), 'Mr Irwin says' (line 32) – repetition of his name to make her feel inadequate • 'It's cutting-edge, miss.' (line 35) – implying that her lessons were not	6	up to 6 marks for three well-chosen quotations with explanations

5.	(a)
	
	(b)
	
	(c)
		they want to know about his personal life
		
		'Are we your life?' (line 45)
		
		if he says yes, they are his life:
		• they will have little respect for him
		• they will think he is a failure in life
		• he will have no mystery
		• they think they will be able to be in control
		
		if he says no, they are not his life/ disregards the question:
		• they will have greater respect for him
		• they will think he is more interesting
		• he will retain control
		• there is more to find out about him
			1
			
			1
			
			4
				1 mark
				
				1 mark
				
				up to 4 marks for well-reasoned points

TOTAL			**25**	

10. *The History Boys* by Alan Bennett

Level 2

Q	Answer	Mark	Additional guidance
1.	Mrs Lintott: • 'battery chicken' (line 9) – the boys are like chickens, cooped up/in a restricted space/body and brains have no freedom/ they have no choice about what they learn • 'You've force-fed us the facts' (line 12) – lessons driven by learning facts, without discussion, with no freedom Mr Irwin: • teaches by allowing the pupils to be 'free-range' (line 8) – he allows them freedom of expression and thought to become better thinkers • 'we're in the process of running around acquiring flavour.' (lines 12–13) – discussion/thinking time/freedom allowed to become more rounded students	4	up to 2 marks for identification of metaphor, each time, and explanation of its implication
2.	polite/agreeable/friendly: • stops him to ask a friendly question about his new teacher – 'How are you all getting on with Mr Irwin?' (line 3) • interested in his answer – 'That's nice to hear' (line 6) rigid/direct teacher: • teaches using facts/explains things methodically/no freedom within lessons – 'Point A. Point B. Point C.' (line 7) predictable: • teaches in an old-fashioned manner • shocked by/not understanding new teaching methods/ideas • responds as Rudge expects her to self-doubting: • she wonders if she is teaching in the right way/using the right materials	4	up to 4 marks for two well-explained impressions each backed up with a quotation or specific reference to text in own words

59

	pitiful/wistful: • she is sad to think they are having fun in lessons without her – 'Dear me. What fun you must all have.' (line 34) inquisitive: • she wants to know what is going on in the lessons – 'How are you all getting on with Mr Irwin?' (line 3)		
3.	sarcastic: • 'It makes me grateful for your lessons.' (lines 4–5) – by the end of the text we realise he does not mean that, he is only saying what he knows she wants to hear mocking: • 'It's only a metaphor, miss.' (line 10) – he is showing off his knowledge to her to please her/put her down tries to annoy her: • 'I'm just going home now to watch some videos of the *Carry On* films.' (lines 17–18) – he knows this will irritate her as he will appear lazy/uncaring about school work evasive/cagey: • 'You never know with him.' (line 22) – deliberately being vague, because he knows she wants to know more goading her: • '(*he is reading from his notes*)' (lines 24–25) – showing off the very different/better/ pompous teaching he is receiving from Mr Irwin provocative: • 'Mr Irwin said' (line 20), 'Mr Irwin says' (line 24), 'Mr Irwin says' (line 32) – repetition of his name to make her feel inadequate cruel/unkind: • 'It's cutting-edge, miss.' (line 35) – implying that her lessons were not	**6**	up to 6 marks for three well-chosen quotations with explanations

4.	(a)	if they are his life:
		• they will have little respect for him
		• they will think he is a failure in life
		• he will have no mystery
		• they think they will be able to be in control and have the upper hand in the relationship
		
		if they are not his life:
		• they will have greater respect for him
		• they will think he is more interesting
		• he will retain control
		• there is more to find out about him so he retains the upper hand in the relationship
			4	up to 4 marks for understanding both possible effects on the relationship

	(b)	his response: 'Pretty dismal if you are. Because (*giving out books*) these are as dreary as ever.' (line 46–47) indicates: • he is not going to tell them • he is deliberately vague/wants privacy • he does not want them to know • he does not fall for their tricks • he is not going to be distracted from the lesson • he is being clever • he is playing them at their own game his behaviour: • he is getting on with the lesson • he is not going to be distracted from the lesson • he is expressing his strong opinion about their books	3	answers should comment on words and behaviour for 3 marks
5.		• 'The wrong end of the stick is the right one.' (line 51) – when you think you have the incorrect answer, it could turn out to be the truth/the right answer • 'A question has a front door and a back door.' (lines 51–52) – there are two ways of looking at the same thing/the question • 'Go in the back, or better still, the side.' (line 52) – there is a third way too, which may be even better	4	up to 2 marks for each thoughtfully explained quotation (candidate may refer to writing techniques within answer)

	• 'Flee the crowd.' (line 53) – do not do the same as everyone else • 'It's a performance. It's entertainment. And if it isn't, make it so.' (line 58) – make your writing engaging/interesting/ make the dull sides of history exciting • 'You want us to find an angle' (line 59) – you want us to do it differently to others/ look at it from an unusual perspective		
TOTAL		**25**	

Paper 1 Section A:
Reading – Poetry

1. 'Paint Box' by Phoebe Hesketh

Level 1

Q	Answer	Mark	Additional guidance
1.	some years ago: • 'The schoolroom' (line 12) • 'blackboard' (line 14) • 'painting-book alphabet' (line 16) • '"You must learn to read," they said/and gave him a painting-book alphabet.' (lines 15–16)	2	two clues needed for 2 marks
2.	'Sunday's white paper' (line 3) • his day appears clear/free to do with as he wants and he likes to be free • his day and mood is peaceful/calm as no one is telling him what to do, as he gets enough of this at school 'shading to grey' (line 3) • starting to feel sad as the day wears on and Sunday, his play day, is nearly over • dreading Monday looming as he does not like school • he is a home-loving boy 'bright yellow brass/of a cock crowing' (lines 5–6) • he finds the sound of the cock crowing is harsh like an alarm clock to signal the day/he does not want to get up to go to school 'Story-time, purple.' (line 7) • he likes story time as the school day is almost over • he likes the comfort of story time as it reminds him of home and nothing is expected of him 'Scarlet is shouting in the playground.' (line 8) • the voices in the playground are harsh sounds in his ear and he is confused and afraid	6	must identify three colours and relate them to boy

		• or he enjoys playtime and is happy to be outside/playing, enjoying the freedom/ letting off steam		
3.	(a)	• metaphor • simile	**2**	1 mark for each identification
		• 'His world's a cocoon' (line 9) – metaphor – his world is safe, within a bubble/he feels restricted and wants to spread his wings • 'round as an egg' (line 10) – simile – no sharp edges, nothing to harm him, easy to fit in	**1**	1 mark for explanation of one of the techniques
	(b)	• 'the enemy blackboard' (line 14) • the school is against him • he is in opposition with school/learning • school/learning is all a fight	**2**	1 mark for identification 1 mark for explanation
4.		• 'square and hard' (line 12) • 'hard and square' (line 13) • words repeated and/or reversed to emphasise that both the schoolroom and his desk are uninviting, whichever way he looks at it • there is no escape from the discomfort • the sharp angles are digging into him • contrasts with comfort of cocoon/egg	**2**	1 mark for 'square' and 'hard' 1 mark for understanding reason for repetition/ reversal
5.	(a)	• 'Apple swelled beautifully red.' (line 17) – he was filling the page quickly and with confidence • 'red' (line 17) and 'blue' (line 18) – he is using strong colours as he is feeling content • 'Balloon/expanded in blue.' (lines 17–18) – he filled the outline of the balloon quickly and confidently	**3**	1 mark for quotation up to 2 marks for explanation of choice
	(b)	• 'C was a cage for a bird' (line 19) – he is beginning to feel trapped • 'his brush wavered through' (line 20) – he is beginning to falter and is not feeling so confident	**3**	1 mark for quotation up to 2 marks for explanation of choice

65

	• 'a small brown smudge inside' (line 22) – he sees himself as insignificant/unimportant/ dull within his imprisoned environment			
6.	• he communicates only through colour: 'He tried to tell them what he felt,/could say it only in colours…' (lines 1–2) • he sees life/lives his life through colour • colour marks out the day and the time of day • colour marks out his activities/moods • 'Paint Box' implies a selection of different colours/moods each compartmentalised • 'Paint Box' implies that his life has parameters and boundaries	**4**	marker's discretion at least two different and thoughtful reasons for 4 marks fewer points in more detail/more points in less detail	
TOTAL		**25**		

1. 'Paint Box' by Phoebe Hesketh

Level 2

Q	Answer	Mark	Additional guidance
1.	'Sunday's white paper' (line 3) • his day appears clear/free to do with as he wants • his day and mood is peaceful/calm as no one is telling him what to do 'shading to grey' (line 3) • oncoming sadness as the day wears on and Sunday is over • a grey mood as Monday looming and he dreads school • his once clear, empty day fills up 'bright yellow brass/of a cock crowing' (lines 5–6) • brash/too bright as the sound of crowing is like an alarm clock to signal the day 'Story-time, purple.' (line 7) • deep/warm/comforting/reminds him of home • school day almost over • nothing is expected of him 'Scarlet is shouting in the playground.' (line 8) • anger/confusion at the loud voices • happy to be outside/playing, enjoying the freedom/letting off steam	6	must identify three colours and explain boy's feelings/ moods, and possible reasons, in detail
2.	• metaphor: 'His world's a cocoon' (line 9) – his own world is safe, within a bubble/ he feels restricted and wants to spread his wings • simile: 'round as an egg' (line 10) – his own world is comfortable with no sharp edges and nothing to harm him/he feels nurtured • metaphor: 'an acorn/sprouting green.' (lines 10–11) – at home he sees himself as able to grow and full of life	6	up to 6 marks for three poetic techniques identified, quoted and explained

	• metaphor: 'The schoolroom square and hard' (line 12) – at school he is not comfortable, with corners and edges which are unforgiving/restricting • repetition: 'The schoolroom square and hard,/his desk hard and square' (lines 12–13) – emphasises that both the schoolroom and his desk are uninviting, whichever way you look at it/there is no escape from the discomfort/the sharp angles are digging into him • metaphor/personification: 'facing the enemy blackboard.' (line 14) – he feels that the school is against him/he is in opposition with school/learning		
3.	he feels confident/relaxed: • 'swelled beautifully' (line 17) 'expanded' (line 18) – his way of painting shows that he is confident/not holding back • 'beautifully red' (line 17), 'Balloon/expanded in blue.' (lines 17–18) – he uses strong colours when painting • enjambment suggests he is painting fast • alliteration of explosive 'b' sound suggests pace and confidence	3	1 mark for mood/feeling up to 2 marks for supporting quotation(s) and explanation some candidates may refer to poet's craft
4.	• the 'cage' (line 19) seems to represent his school life where he feels trapped • 'his brush wavered' (line 20) as he comes to paint the cage because he hesitates as he thinks he is like the imprisoned bird • he is 'a small brown smudge inside' (line 22) – he considers himself to be thought of as unimportant/insignificant and dull within that world	6	up to 6 marks for understanding: 'cage'/imprisonment 'wavered'/realisation that he sees himself in the picture 'small brown smudge'/himself
5.	• poet shows the reader that the boy's life is represented by a paint box • the character is anonymous, only pronouns used, except for a range of different feelings represented by the colours in the paint box	4	marker's discretion two different and thoughtful reasons for 4 marks or fewer points in more detail

	• he communicates only through colour: 'He tried to tell them what he felt/could say it only in colours...' (lines 1–2) • he sees life and lives his life through colour • colour marks out the day and the time of day • colour marks out/represents his activities/ moods • 'Paint Box' implies a selection of different colours/moods, each compartmentalised • 'Paint Box' implies that his life has parameters and boundaries		
TOTAL		**25**	

2. 'Fox' by Ted Hughes

Level 1

Q		Answer	Mark	Additional guidance
1.	(a)	• Checks his watch by the stars' (line 3) • 'And letting one fang wink in the moonlight' (line 18) • 'Shows us the moon' (line 20)	2	two quotations needed 1 mark for each quotation
	(b)	• hen • pheasant • gander/goose	3	1 mark for each
2.	(a)	• 'smartest evening dress' (line 2) • 'white-scarfed' (line 4) • 'To the opera' (line 5) • 'conduct the orchestra' (line 7)	2	two quotations needed for 2 marks
	(b)	• to draw attention to the fox's dark eyes • because Robin Hood stole from the rich • as a disguise • because he will trick the pheasant as he will keep the spoils for himself	2	up to two reasons depending on detail
	(c)	• 'Flinging back his Dracula cloak' (line 17) – wears a black, magic coat • 'Lifts off his top hat' (line 19) – using his top hat to show off to his audience • 'Then brings out of it, in a flourish of feathers' (line 21) – produces his magic out of his hat	2	one relevant quotation with explanation needed for 2 marks
3.		• 'opera' (line 5) – hen house is like a noisy opera house with orchestra tuning up and hens squawking nervously • 'gold' (line 12) – the golden feathers of the dead pheasant are his treasure	4	up to 4 marks for explanation of both
4.		stanza one: cunning/sly/keen/enthusiastic/trickster: • 'Where he will conduct the orchestra' (line 7) – he will organise and control the hens in order to kill them	6	impression, quotation and explanation needed from each stanza

	• 'Checks his watch by the stars' (line 3) – understands his mission/eager to get on with the job • 'And hurries' (line 4) – keen to hunt stanza two: merciless/cruel/heartless/ruthless/smug: • 'silent laughter' (line 11) – cruel/ruthless as he is going to kill • 'Shakes all the gold out of his robes' (line 12) – smug/pleased with his haul/kill • 'Then carries him bodily home' (line 13) – pleased with his catch • 'A swag-bag?' (line 15) – merciless pleasure at his haul • 'Over his shoulder' (line 14) – heartless about the dead creature stanza three: flashy/showy/cheeky/entertaining: • 'Flinging back his Dracula cloak' (line 17) – flashy/showy/grand movement as if he is a showman • 'lifts off his top hat' (line 19) – grand gesture of entertainer • 'Then brings out of it, in a flourish of feathers' (line 21) – cheeky/flashy/gesture of success • 'One fang wink in the moonlight' (line 18) – cheeky/pleased with himself/showing off • 'Shows us the moon through the bottom of it' (line 20) – flashy/cheeky/entertaining his audience		
5.	yes, to be admired: • he is clever/outwits the other creatures • he plans/hunts craftily • he is successful every time • he is shown to be grand in his clothing and gestures no, not to be admired: • he is unfeeling/disrespectful of life • he is cruel/ruthless • he is sly/cunning/plays tricks • he gloats in his success	4	reward quality of arguments and reference to text candidate does not need to argue both sides, but does need to provide own opinion for full marks
TOTAL		25	

2. 'Fox' by Ted Hughes

Level 2

Q	Answer	Mark	Additional guidance
1.	• at night • fowl/birds • hen • pheasant • gander/goose	2	1 mark 1 mark for collective noun for all or each bird to be identified
2.	stanza one: conductor: • 'smartest evening dress' (line 2) – dressed like a conductor • 'white-scarfed' (line 4) – dressed like a conductor • 'To the opera' (line 5) – explains the work he is going to do • 'conduct the orchestra?' (line 7) – explains the work he is going to do stanza two: Robin Hood/robber/burglar: • 'Robin Hood mask over his eyes' (line 9) – dark markings around fox's eyes/disguise to trick as he will keep spoils for himself • 'Shakes all the gold out of his robes' (line 12) – he reveals all the treasure from thefeathers of the pheasant • 'A swag-bag?' (line 15) – the bag a robber uses to carry the haul stanza three: magician: • 'Flinging back his Dracula cloak (line 17) – wears a black cloak like a magician • 'Lifts off his top hat' (line 19) – wears a top hat like a magician • 'Shows us the moon through the bottom of it' (line 20) – magician's gesture to show no trickery	6	up to 2 marks for each identity, quotation and explanation Dracula not acceptable as an identity

	• 'Then brings out of it, in a flourish of feathers,/The gander' (lines 21–22) – produces bird as if by magic		
3.	stanza one: confident: • 'Where he will conduct the orchestra?' (line 7) – he will organise and control the hens/he behaves with authority over his victims impatient: • 'Checks his watch by the stars' (line 3) – understands his mission/eager to get on with the job/works with understanding/ has a plan excited: • 'And hurries' (line 4) – keen to hunt/ hungry for success stanza two: cruel/merciless/mean/ruthless/triumphant: • 'silent laughter' (line 11) – amused as he is going to kill/feeling of inward triumph proud/smug: • 'Shakes all the gold out of his robes' (line 12) – pleased with his haul • 'Then carries him bodily home' (line 13) – pleased with his catch/no respect for his victim • 'A swag-bag?'(line 15) – pleased with his haul uncaring: • 'Over his shoulder' (line 14) – not caring for the dead creature/disrespectful towards the dead stanza three: bold/confident/buoyant: • 'Flinging back his Dracula cloak' (line 17) – grand movement/showing off • 'Lifts off his top hat' (line 19) – grand gesture/playing to his audience • 'Then brings out of it, in a flourish of feathers' (line 21) – gesture of success	6	three insightful feelings with evidence and explanation for 6 marks

	• 'Shows us the moon through the bottom of it' (line 20) – entertaining his audience in overconfident/flamboyant way cheeky/mischievous: • 'one fang wink in the moonlight' (line 18) – pleased with himself/showing off		
4.	the use of repetition: • 'who' is repeated at the beginning of each stanza – each time a question is opened in the same way • slows down the pace of the poem at that point • emphasises that the fox is a mysterious creature the use of questions: • the whole poem is a series of questions which keeps the reader focused on the fox • they engage the reader and keep the reader interested • each stanza begins with 'who' so that you are forced to read on to hear the rest of the question • repetition of questions signifies the increasing daring of the fox the use of imagery: • gives the reader a very visual picture of the fox • 'white-scarfed' (line 4) – metaphor – white chest emphasised • 'opera' (line 5) – metaphor – a place you visit in the evening full of bustle and noise • 'orchestra' (line 7) – metaphor – noisy group making different sounds, waiting for leadership • 'Robin Hood mask' (line 9) – metaphor/personification – dark markings around fox's eyes/disguise to trick as he will keep spoils for himself	**6**	up to 2 marks for identifying and explaining effect of repetition up to 2 marks for explaining effects of questions up to 2 marks for identifying and explaining effect of imagery

	• 'king Pheasant the Magnificent' (line 10) – personification – emphasises that the fox will outwit/bring down even the greatest/most impressive • 'gold' (line 12) – metaphor – pheasant's beautiful/precious feathers • 'swag-bag' (line 15) – metaphor – dead pheasant is his large haul • 'Dracula cloak' (line 17) – metaphor/personification – black cloak suggesting menace • 'fang' (line 18) – metaphor – killer canine tooth revealed		
5.	yes, to be admired: • he is cunning/outwits the other creatures • he outwits humans who took protective action to lock up the goose • he plans/hunts craftily at the best time • he is confident in his success every time • he is shown to be grand in his clothing and gestures no, not to be admired: • he is unfeeling/disrespectful of life • he is cruel/ruthless • he is sly/cunning/plays tricks • he gloats in his success own opinion based on above arguments	5	reward quality of arguments and reference to text candidate does not need to argue both sides, but does need to provide own opinion for full marks
TOTAL		25	

3. 'Frustration' by Tom Earley

Level 1

Q		Answer	Mark	Additional guidance
1.		usually: • they sunbathe • they are huddling down on the grass to keep warm • sitting as though on a nest/eggs now: • they are standing stiff and motionless • all looking in the same direction • with their heads stretched upwards and necks taut	4	up to 2 marks for each explanation of contrasting behaviours/postures must be in own words for full marks
2.	(a)	• 'His black body was pressed …/As flat as a plate.' (lines 11–12) – his body lies close/horizontal/levelled out to the ground, so as not to be seen • 'He eased himself forward like a snake.' (line 15) – he carefully moves/slides forward, silently and stealthily	2	1 mark for quotation 1 mark for description of image
	(b)	• 'mouth mimed' – alliteration • 'mimed' – personification • 'inaudible cries' – oxymoron	1	1 mark for identification of one technique
		• his mouth opens and closes as if to make a threatening miaow, but no sound is heard/comes out, as he is stalking prey	2	up to 2 marks for explanation of whole sentence/quotation
3.	(a)	• there is first a short sentence – creates tension/the reader pauses, as if to hold breath too • there is next a long sentence over four lines – it makes you read the lines more quickly as the cat springs and pounces • enjambment – where the meaning runs on over the lines – provides pace as the reader does not pause	2 + 2	2 marks for recognition of short sentence and explanation of effect 2 marks for recognition of long sentence and explanation of effect (recognition of enjambment not necessary)

	(b)	• 'no hostage/Left, no victim.' (lines 19–20) – emphasises that the cat catches nothing	2	1 mark for quoting repetition 1 mark for explanation of effect
4.		• 'no hostage/Left, no victim.' (lines 19–20) – the cat fails in its attempt to catch a bird • 'The cats's angry tail slashed the turf.' (line 21) – the cat is furious that it has failed to catch a bird	4	two quotations with explanations needed for 4 marks
5.	(a)	'A hunting cat poised for the kill.' (line 10) – the poet thinks that the cat will be the winner/catch a pigeon as it is: • 'A hunting cat' (line 10) – predator/ recognition of killer cat • 'poised for the kill' (line 10) – ready and well-positioned for the kill	4	up to 2 marks for the complete quotation up to 2 marks for explanation of two phrases from quotation
	(b)	• the poet is intrigued/wants to watch the hunt to its conclusion • the poet does not want to interfere with nature • it happened so quickly there was no chance to intervene • the poet does not know what he can do	2	up to 2 marks for one explained reasonable suggestion
TOTAL			25	

3. 'Frustration' by Tom Earley

Level 2

Q	Answer	Mark	Additional guidance
1.	usually: • they sunbathe • they are huddling down on the grass to keep warm • sitting as though on a nest/eggs now: • they are standing stiff and motionless • all looking in the same direction, with their heads stretched upwards and necks taut	4	up to 2 marks for explanations of both contrasting behaviours/ postures must be in own words for full marks
2.	• 'black body' (line 11) – alliteration – emphasises colour/evil • 'His black body was pressed …/As flat as a plate.' (lines 11–12) – simile – his body lies close/horizontal/levelled out to the ground, so as not to be seen • 'mouth mimed' (line 14) – alliteration – the repeated 'm' sound suggests a miaow sound • 'mimed' (line 14) – personification – as if he is pretending/acting out threatening noise • 'inaudible cries' (line 14) – oxymoron – contradictory phrase which emphasises that despite the cry being silent it is still threatening • 'He eased himself forward like a snake.' (line 15) – simile – he carefully moves/ slides forward, silently and stealthily	6	up to 6 marks for quotation, identification, and explanation of three poetic techniques
3.	• 'I held my breath.' (line 17) – short sentence – creates tension waiting for the pounce/the reader pauses, as if to hold breath too • 'I did not see him spring,/Only heard the explosion of wings/And saw the massed flight: no hostage/Left, no victim.' (lines 17–20) – long sentence over four lines – makes you read the lines with pace/	6	up to 2 marks for each writing device quoted, identified and explained

		mirroring the action as the cat springs and pounces for the kill • enjambment – where the meaning runs on over the lines – provides pace as the reader does not pause • caesura – breaks the rhythm – to emphasise the tension at the crisis • 'no hostage/Left, no victim.' (lines 19–20) – repetition – emphasises that the cat fails/ catches nothing • 'explosion' (line 18), 'hostage' (line 19), 'victim' (line 20) – extended metaphor which emphasises the war/fight/what might have been	25	
4.	(a)	the poet thinks that the cat will be the winner/catch a pigeon as it is: • 'behind the birds' (line 9) – cunning positioning • 'alarmingly close' (line 9) – so close that it must be able to catch a pigeon • 'A hunting cat' (line 10) – predator/ recognition of killer cat • 'poised for the kill' (line 10) – ready and well-positioned for the kill	3	1 mark for each explained quotation
	(b)	the cat is frustrated because: • 'no hostage/Left, no victim.' (lines 19–20) – the cat fails in its attempt to catch a bird • 'The cat's angry tail slashed the turf.' (line 21) – the cat is furious that it has failed to catch a bird	2	up to 2 marks for understanding of cat's frustration, with relevant quotation/s
5.		mood in first sentence: • comforting/relaxed/peaceful mood in last sentence: • angry/tormented • effective as reader lulled in opening/is given setting details/not expecting what is to come • contrasts with dramatic end/brings it to a conclusion/detail of cat's anger/frustration	4	up to 1–2 marks for understanding of mood up to 2–3 marks for reasonable suggestions
TOTAL			**25**	

4. 'Flag' by John Agard

Level 1

Q		Answer	Mark	Additional guidance
1.	(a)	• each stanza begins with a question in line 1 • lines 2 and 3 answer the question	2	1 mark for noticing 'question' 1 mark for noticing 'answer'
	(b)	• 'What's that' • 'It's just a piece of cloth/that'	2	two examples to be given
2.		• 'that makes the guts of men grow bold.' (line 6) – the sight of the flag makes men become brave as they remember what they are fighting for • 'that dares the coward to relent.' (line 9) – the sight of the flag challenges anyone to give up the fight or surrender and so ensures people continue to fight • 'that will outlive the blood you bleed.' (line 12) – the flag will remain constant and still be there despite injury or death	2 2 2	up to 2 marks for explaining each example of personification
3.	(a)	• 'unfurling' (line 4) means that it unwraps itself from the pole • 'rising' (line 7) means that it moves up the pole/upwards into the air • 'flying' (line 10) means that it is fully open and streaming in the air	3	all three words to be identified and explained in own words
	(b)	stanza two: • the flag-pole is in a place where men are rallying/meeting, e.g. street, army camp, field stanza three: • the flag is over a tent which is within an assembly point/army camp/base, possibly where war is imminent	3	accept any sensible response which displays understanding

		stanza four: • the flag is flying over the battlefield/carried by horses, urging on the troops		
4.	(a)	• he wants to have something that seems to be so powerful • he wants to be part of the mission/join up • he wants to be brave/prove himself • it is something small and simple that has a lot of meaning	3	up to 3 marks for any sensible responses which indicate understanding
	(b)	• you are stuck/trapped/have allegiance to your new cause • you may feel morally guilty at your actions, as a man, despite the cause	2	up to 2 marks for any sensible response which indicates understanding
5.		agree: • it is, literally, a piece of cloth • it can be burnt or destroyed easily/is not lasting • does not have any power of its own disagree: • the flag can be a symbol to unite powerful forces, e.g. crown, war, countries, troops or to unify a group of people • creates a sense of identity • people/causes give the flag power	4	up to 4 marks for two sensible responses, either in agreement or disagreement or both
TOTAL			25	

4. 'Flag' by John Agard

Level 2

Q		Answer	Mark	Additional guidance
1.	(a)	patterns: • a question followed by an answer • two different voices • repetition • regular rhythm • regular rhyme • the shape of the stanza is always the same • each stanza consists of three lines • the middle line is always shorter	4	1 mark for each
	(b)	• the nature of the question changes • reveals what the 'piece of cloth' is • reveals consequences of owning it • the answering voice is stronger/more powerful/direct • repetition ends/stops • rhyme scheme changes	2	2 marks for two observations rhythm stays the same, so not relevant the shape stays the same, so not relevant
2.		personification • 'that makes the guts of men grow bold.' (line 6) – it enables/steels men to become brave/courageous • 'that dares the coward to relent.' (line 9) – it challenges anyone weak to give up the fight or surrender • 'that will outlive the blood you bleed.' (line 12) – the cause will continue even after personal injury or death	4	1 mark 1 mark for explaining understanding each time
3.	(a)	stanza two: • 'unfurling' (line 4) means that it unwraps itself from the pole • the flag-pole is in a place where men are rallying/meeting, e.g. street, army camp, field	6	1 mark for each stanza, word/participle to be identified and explained in own words

		stanza three: • 'rising' (line 7) means that it moves up the pole/upwards into the air • the flag is over a tent which is within an assembly point/army camp/base, possibly where war is imminent stanza four: • 'flying' (line 10) means that it is fully open and streaming in the air • the flag is flying over the battlefield/carried by horses, urging on the troops		each scene beneath to be described for 1 mark accept any thoughtful response which displays understanding
	(b)	• as the flag unfolds, expands and flies so the battle escalates below • the height and movement of the flag is symbolic of the intensity of activity below	2	2 marks for reference to flag and activity which demonstrates understanding of parallel
4.	(a)	• he wants to have something that seems to be so powerful • he wants to be part of the mission/join up • he wants to be brave/prove himself • it is something small and simple that has a lot of meaning	1	1 mark for any response which indicates understanding
	(b)	• you are stuck/trapped/have allegiance to your new cause for ever • you may always feel morally guilty for your actions, as a man, despite the cause • you will need to restrict your moral sensibility/outlook until death if in possession of the flag	2	up to 2 marks for responses which indicate understanding
5.		agree: • it is a piece of cloth • it is mass produced • it can be burnt or destroyed easily/is not lasting • does not have any power of its own disagree: • the flag can be a symbol to unite powerful forces, e.g. crown, war, countries, troops or to unify a group of people	4	at marker's discretion up to 4 marks for two considered responses, either in agreement or disagreement or both

	• creates a sense of identity • people/causes give the flag power some candidates may include additional analysis of language: • monosyllabic/simplistic vocabulary • repetition of phrase 'It's just a piece of cloth' • 'just' – meaning 'only' • contrast of simple idea with significance of the following line		
TOTAL		**25**	

5. 'The Caged Bird in Springtime' by James Kirkup

Level 1

Q		Answer	Mark	Additional guidance
1.	(a)	the bird is worried/anxious/confused about being caged/not free/unable to do what instinct is telling it to do	1	1 mark for understanding reason for bird's questions
	(b)	• 'This curious anxiety?' (line 2) • 'But how absurd!' (line 5) • 'And I do not know/What flying means' (lines 7–8) • 'I cannot quite remember how/It is done' (lines 14–15) • 'weep with anguish' (line 20) • 'beat my head' (line 21)	2	up to 2 marks for two words/phrases reward best/strongest quotations
2.		• fly • build a nest fly: • 'It is as if I wanted/To fly away from here.' (lines 3–4) • 'I have never flown in my life' (line 6) • 'And I do not know/What flying means' (lines 7–8) build a nest: • 'But I want to build my own' (line 12) • 'I know/That what I want to do/Cannot be done here.' (lines 15–17)	4	1 mark for each 1 mark for suitable/ supporting quotation 1 mark for suitable/ supporting quotation
3.	(a)	• 'weep' – the bird is sorrowfully crying in distress • 'anguish' – his cry is one of suffering/pain/ torment • 'beat' – frustration/desperation to get out/ agony of being trapped • 'sharp' – feels pain	3	three words to be explained
	(b)	• 'Smile' – happy/entertained/oblivious • 'Hark how he sings' – amused/showing enjoyment/unaware of the real reason for his song	3	up to 2 marks for explanations/observations of vocabulary choices

		• the words used to describe the bird are negative and harsh, whereas the words to describe the children are positive/happy		1 mark for awareness of contrast
4.		advantages for bird in the cage: • own ideas: safety, protection, no predators, warmth • from text: seeds/food, water, air, light disadvantages for bird if free: • predators, cold/weather, struggle to find food/water, struggle to find shelter	6	up to 3 marks for well-explained advantages responses must include own ideas in addition to ideas from text up to 3 marks for well-explained disadvantages
5.	(a)	• it is wrong to cage birds • instinct will always prevail • birds should be able to fly and build nests • no bird can feel natural when it is caged • animals/birds are not here for human entertainment • it is not enough to give food, water, air and light in exchange for its captivity • humans should respect birds'/animals' rights and instincts	4	up to 4 marks for two relevant and explained suggestions
	(b)	agree: • birds should always be in their natural habitat despite inherent dangers • it is not for humans to decide where birds live • it is cruel to restrict/prevent birds' flight and need to nest disagree: • there may be times when it is advisable to keep birds in captivity, e.g. to prevent extinction, veterinary care, research, education, bird sanctuary	2	up to 2 marks for a well-reasoned and sensible answer
TOTAL			**25**	

5. 'The Caged Bird in Springtime' by James Kirkup

Level 2

Q	Answer	Mark	Additional guidance
1.	• the questions engage the reader/draw the reader in • each new question allows the reader to think from the bird's point of view • the bird's attempt to answer its own questions creates a pattern • the bird is worried/anxious/confused • it tries to answer its own questions which emphasises its helplessness	4	up to 2 marks for response which shows understanding of question and answer structure up to 2 marks for response which shows understanding of the bird
2.	• unable to fly • unable to build a nest • instinct is trying to prevail • it wants to behave as it would if free/in the wild • instinct especially strong in springtime	4	1 mark for each up to 2 marks for answers which reflect understanding of instinct
3.	bird negative, emotive, sad words: • 'weep' – the bird is sorrowfully crying in distress/crying bitterly • 'anguish' – his cry is one of suffering/pain/torment • 'beat' – frustration/desperation to escape/agony of being trapped • 'sharp' – feels pain children positive, happy words/phrases: • 'Smile' – cheerful/entertained/oblivious • 'Hark how he sings' – amused/showing enjoyment/unaware of the real reason for his song • deliberate vocabulary choices to show contrast in mood between bird and children • children's misunderstanding of bird's situation shows irony	6	candidates should comment on the general mood of the word choices in each case comment in detail on at least one word/phrase for each understanding of contrast necessary for full marks reward candidates who identify irony

4.	(a)	• metaphor	3	1 mark
		• to emphasise that to the bird the branches are hidden • to emphasise that the branches will always be elusive to the bird • to emphasise that the branches will always be unknown to the bird		up to 2 marks for explanation showing understanding
	(b)	• simple, like the bird's mind • poignant in its simplicity • childlike which makes the poem very accessible	3	up to 3 marks for reasonable suggestions
5.		• despite the caged bird having what it needs to live, it is denied a natural life • it is not enough to provide the caged bird with food, water, air and light • it is wrong to cage birds under any circumstances • animals/birds are not here for human entertainment • instinct will always prevail agree: • birds should always be in their natural habitat despite inherent dangers disagree: • there may be times when it is advisable to keep birds in captivity, e.g. to prevent extinction, veterinary care, research, education, bird sanctuary	5	marker's discretion depending on detail given up to 2/3 marks for understanding of message up to 2/3 marks for own opinion based on the poem
TOTAL			**25**	

6. 'Going for Water' by Robert Frost

Level 1

Q		Answer	Mark	Additional guidance
1.		• 'The well was dry beside the door' (line 1) – there had been so little rain that even the well had dried up • 'To seek the brook if still it ran' (line 4) – there had been so little rain that even the brook/stream might have dried up	4	two quotations with explanations needed for 4 marks
2.	(a)	• 'Not loth to have excuse to go' (line 5)	2	2 marks for identification of quotation
	(b)	• the weather that evening was good, despite a little cold • they feel they own the fields/woods	2	2 marks for two different reasons
3.		stanza three: • 'We ran as if to meet the moon' (line 9) – running excitedly/happily/freely/with expectation into the open space stanza four: • 'Ready to run to hiding new/With laughter' (lines 15–16) – enjoying the pretend game of hide and seek stanza five: • 'Each laid on other a staying hand' (line 17) – they stopped each other from running on • 'To listen ere we dared to look' (line 18) – careful to listen for sounds of the brook/stream before they looked for it	3 + 3	three quotations with explanation needed for 6 marks
4.	(a)	• tinkling' (line 22) • the stream/brook makes a soft gentle sound of flowing water	2	1 mark for identification 1 mark for explanation
	(b)	simile	1	1 mark for identification
	(c)	metaphor	1	1 mark for identification
		'the water is now a silvery colour, in the moonlight, and is smooth/long/solid	2	up to 2 marks for explanation of picture, depending on detail

89

5.	(a)	• rhyme • second and fourth lines rhyme	2	up to 2 marks for noticing rhyme and the pattern
	(b)	• regular rhythm • four beats to a line	2	up to 2 marks for noticing rhythm and the pattern
	(c)	the rhythm and the rhyme make you read the poem quickly and steadily/moves it along speedily	1	1 mark for reasonable answer
TOTAL			**25**	

6. 'Going for Water' by Robert Frost

Level 2

Q	Answer	Mark	Additional guidance
1.	bored: • 'Not loth to have excuse to go' (line 5) – pleased to have a reason to go to the brook happy: • 'Because the autumn eve was fair/(Though chill)' (lines 6–7) – pleased to go out as a fine evening proud/enjoying their own land: • 'because the fields were ours,/And by the brook our woods were there.' (lines 7–8) – they felt as if they owned the fields and woods on the way to the brook	4	two feelings, explained and supported, for 4 marks
2.	• 'the moon/That slowly dawned behind the trees' (lines 9–10) – metaphor/word play – emphasises that the trees are without leaves as the moon can be seen behind them • 'The barren boughs' (line 11) – alliteration – explosive/repeated 'b' sound emphasises that the branches are without leaves as it is autumn • 'The barren boughs' (line 11) – metaphor – emphasises that the branches of the trees are without life/are not able to produce leaves/fruit as it is autumn • 'without the leaves,/Without the birds, without the breeze.' (lines 11–12) – repetition – emphasises the autumnal emptiness and stillness of the wood • triple rhyme (unexpected) of trees/leaves/breeze reminds reader of freeze and contributes with long ee sound to emphasise the effect of cold	6	up to 2/3 marks for two/three quotations with identification and explanation of poetic techniques

3.	reasons for it being a turning point: mood/children's behaviour changes from being playful/happy to cautious/pensive/ nervous anticipation:	5	up to 5 marks, depending on detail, for recognising and explaining one/two relevant reasons for it being a turning point
	• 'Each laid on other a staying hand' (line 17) – the children now stop each other/draw to a halt • 'To listen ere we dared to look' (line 18) – they need to be quiet to try to hear the brook/they are scared/nervous of what they might find as the brook might have dried up • 'And in the hush we joined to make' (line 19) – together they add to the quietness around them they have found what they are looking for: • 'We heard, we knew we heard the brook.' (line 20) – excitement as the brook is still flowing/repetition of 'we heard' emphasises their joy at finding the brook/ the reason for their journey		awareness of change necessary in answer
4.	• 'tinkling' (line 22) – onomatopoeia – the stream/brook makes a soft gentle sound of flowing water • 'a slender tinkling' (line 22) – metaphor and onomatopoeia – slight sound of flowing water • 'drops that floated on the pool/Like pearls' (lines 23–24) – simile – round/pale/ smooth/separate beads of water • 'and now a silver blade.' (line 24) – metaphor – the water is now a silvery colour, in the moonlight, and is smooth/ long/solid	6	three techniques to be quoted, identified and explained
5.	rhyme: • regular • second and fourth lines rhyme	4	marker's discretion recognition of patterns of rhythm and rhyme needed for 2 marks

	rhythm: • regular rhythm • four beats/stresses to a line • eight syllables to a line effective because: • they create pace as you read to the end of the lines • they create predictability • they are comforting • they are song-like/musical • moves along quickly and steadily • flows like the water in the brook		reasons for effectiveness of rhythm and rhyme can be explained separately (1 mark each) or together (2 marks)
TOTAL		**25**	

7. 'The Hermit' by W H Davies

Level 1

Q		Answer	Mark	Additional guidance
1.	(a)	stanza one: • waves • thunder stanza two: • oak tree • lightning striking an oak tree • crack of a frozen pond when melting	2	1 mark for each, in either own words or quotation
	(b)	stanza three: • blind bat taps • small bird in the leaves stanza four: • moths on his pillow • mouse inside the walls	2	1 mark for each, in either own words or quotation
	(c)	• loud noises not frightening but small noises are • nature outside not threatening but inside house is • small animal sounds more frightening than the sounds of the elements • he feels safer outside than inside	3	list not required: summary of contrast needed 1 mark for each reasonable suggestion best candidates will notice three things
2.		• 'boom' (line 1) – can hear the loud low crash of the waves • 'roar' (line 3) – can hear the loud growl of the thunder • 'groan' (line 5) – can hear the low moaning of the tree • 'taps' (line 9) – can hear a light, short sound • 'crunching' (line 16) – can hear the harsh gravelly sound of the tiger walking	4	1 mark for each quotation 1 mark for each explanation
3.	(a)	that is how the bird seems to the man – emphasises its imagined size – contrast of size/ferocity between bird and beast	1	reward any appropriate comments

	(b)	'Comes like a tiger crunching through the stones' (line 16) – enables reader to hear and see the mouse from the hermit's point of view – emphasises his fear as tigers are loud, fierce and huge	**3**	1 mark for simile up to 2 marks for explanation
4.	(a)	• second and fourth lines rhyme • rhyme pattern: abcb	**1**	either form of recognition for 1 mark
	(b)	• semicolon and full stop • semicolon at the end of the second line • full stop at the end of the fourth line/ each stanza	**2**	1 mark for naming both punctuation marks 1 mark for stating where they fall
	(c)	• has a steady pattern like his life • reflects pattern/rhythms of nature • like the repetitive nature of his life • predictable like his life	**1**	1 mark for similar and sensible answer
5.	(a)	• does things alone e.g. walks by sea, in woods, by pond • is alone at night • no talking so quiet sounds emphasised	**2**	or similar – two clues needed
	(b)	*answers may refer to:* yes: • he chooses to be there alone • he likes to be outside • he enjoys nature • he appreciates the elements no: • he is frightened by small noises at night • his imagination plays tricks on him at night	**2**	or similar – two reasons needed yes and/or no response acceptable
	(c)	candidate's own response: answers will vary	**2**	award marks according to quality of response
TOTAL			**25**	

7. 'The Hermit' by W H Davies

Level 2

Q	Answer	Mark	Additional guidance
1. (a)	• waves • thunder • lightning striking tree • pond	2	up to 2 marks for four things either in own words or quotation
(b)	• bat • bird • moth • mouse	2	up to 2 marks for four things either in own words or quotation or similar
(c)	• loud noises are not frightening but small noises are • nature outside is not threatening but inside the house is • small animal sounds are more frightening than the sounds of the elements • he feels safer outside than inside	2	up to 2 marks depending on detail
2.	• 'boom' (line 1) – onomatopoeia – can hear the loud low crash of the waves • 'roar' (line 3) – onomatopoeia – can hear the loud growl of the thunder • 'groan' (line 5) – onomatopoeia/(personification) – can hear the low moaning of the tree • 'bat taps' (line 9) – onomatopoeia and/or assonance – can hear a light, short sound • 'blind bat' (line 9) – alliteration – can hear short explosive sound • 'crunching' (line 16) – onomatopoeia – can hear the harsh gravelly sound of the tiger walking	4	1 mark for each quotation with technique named 1 mark for each explanation
3.	• 'the small bird sounds like some great beast' – that is how the bird seems to the man – it emphasises its imagined huge size/sound • 'Comes like a tiger crunching through the stones' – enables reader to hear and see	4	1 mark for each simile 1 mark for each explanation

		the mouse from the hermit's point of view – emphasises his fear as tigers are loud, fierce and huge		
4.	(a)	• rhythm: regular/steady/has a beat/five stresses per line • rhyme: regular/abcb/last word on second and fourth lines rhyme	4	up to 2 marks for each depending on detail of answer
	(b)	• has a steady pattern like his life • reflects pattern/rhythms of nature • like the repetitive nature of his life • predictable/monotonous like his life	2	two points (or similar) needed
5.	(a)	someone who chooses to live alone in an isolated place/or similar	1	both points needed for 1 mark
	(b)	candidate's own response: answers will vary	2	award marks according to quality of response
	(c)	*answers may refer to:* yes: • he chooses to be there alone • he likes to be outside • he enjoys nature • he appreciates the elements no: • he is frightened by small noises at night • his imagination plays tricks on him at night • sounds are magnified at night	2	or similar – two reasons needed – yes and/or no responses acceptable
TOTAL			**25**	

8. 'Sleet' by Norman MacCaig

Level 1

Q		Answer	Mark	Additional guidance
1.	(a)	• stanza one: sleet • stanza two: snow • stanza three: sleet	1	all needed for 1 mark
	(b)	stanza one: • 'swished heavily' (line 1) – falls with a hissing sound swiftly and thickly • 'couldn't bear to touch/Anything solid' (lines 3–4) – melts as soon as touches anything hard • 'It died' (line 4) – melted completely stanza two: • 'it grins like a maniac' (line 5) – has a smiling/pleasing madness about it • 'It puts a glove on your face.' (line 6) – covers your face warmly **or** is suffocating • 'It stops gaps.' (line 6) – it fills in spaces • 'It catches your eye and your breath' (line 7) – you cannot see or breathe **or** it is striking in its beauty and makes you hold your breath • 'It settles down' (line 7) – covers gently • 'Ponderously crushing trees' (line 8) – mass of snow weighs down branches stanza three: • 'dissolving spiders on cheekbones' (line 9) – melts patterns of cold on face • 'sky filthily weeping' (line 12) – sky crying sadly with dark, dirty tears	6	three verbs or verb phrases (one from each stanza) with explanation of choices necessary for 6 marks
2.	(a)	• personification (also accept alliteration and metaphor)	1	1 mark
	(b)	• 'grins like a maniac in the moon' (line 5)	1	1 mark

	(c)	• metaphor • melting delicate patterns of cold on the face/cold, light feeling as sleet melts on your cheeks	**1** **2**	1 mark up to 2 marks for one similar explanation
3.	(a)	• mixture of short and long sentences • full stops sometimes come in middle of lines • rhythm interrupted/disguised/broken because of varied sentence lengths • rhythm interrupted because of sentence closures mid-line/short sentences	**4**	1 mark for sentence understanding 1 mark for punctuation understanding up to 2 marks for explanation of effect
	(b)	• is one long sentence • rhythm more regular/not interrupted/ disguised/broken	**2**	1 mark 1 mark
4.	(a)	past tense, present tense, past tense	**1**	all three needed for 1 mark
	(b)	*answers may refer to:* • middle stanza has different tense as it contains different subject matter • first and third stanzas are about what he actually saw • middle stanza includes his general opinion/ thoughts about snow	**2**	up to 2 marks for well-reasoned answer
5.		• 'smudging the mind' – mind is blurred/ senses distorted by the sleet • 'That humped itself by the fire' – person sits lethargic/lazily/wrapped up by the fire • 'turning away/From the ill wind' – turning away from cold, windy weather • 'the sky filthily weeping.' – depression inside is reflected in the weather and atmosphere outside	**4**	award 1 mark for each of the four phrases, reasonably explained in own words
TOTAL			**25**	

8. 'Sleet' by Norman MacCaig

Level 2

Q	Answer	Mark	Additional guidance
1. (a)	• sleet: 'swished heavily' (line 1) – falls with a hissing sound swiftly and thickly • snow: 'settles down' (line 7) – covers gently • sleet: 'fine in the wind' (line 3) – lighter than snow, able to be blown • snow: 'puts a glove on your face' (line 6) – covers your face warmly or is suffocating • sleet: 'couldn't bear to touch/Anything solid.' (lines 3–4) – melts as soon as touches anything hard • snow: 'It stops gaps.' (line 6) – it fills in spaces • sleet: 'It died a pauper's death.' (line 4) – melted completely • snow: 'Ponderously crushing trees' (line 8) – mass of snow weighs down branches • snow: 'It catches your eyes and your breath.' (line 7) – you cannot see or breathe or it is striking in its beauty and makes you hold your breath	6	any three differences needed, supported by quotations and explanations
(b)	• mind is blurred/senses distorted by the sleet • become lethargic/sit by the fire • turn away from the weather	3	three summaries needed for 3 marks
2.	stanza one: • 'died a pauper's death' (line 4) – personification/metaphor – never came to anything in life or dies from cold on the streets like a homeless person • 'died a pauper's death' (line 4) – alliteration – repeated heavy 'd' sound emphasises its death through melting	6	up to 2 marks for identifying and explaining one technique in each stanza/line

	stanza two: • 'Ponderously crushing trees with its airy ounces.' (line 8) – metaphor/personification – slowly and heavily causing trees to bend even though snow is so light • 'crushing trees with its airy ounces.' (line 8) – oxymoron – contrast of ideas – makes you wonder why the lightness of snow has such an effect stanza three: • 'the sky filthily weeping.' (line 12) – personification/metaphor – sky crying sadly with dark dirty tears		
3.	• past tense, present tense, past tense • different subject matter in stanza two • stanza two seems to be his general opinion of snow/first and third stanzas are about what was actually happening in the sleet	2	1 mark for tense analysis 1 mark for sensible reason
4.	stanza two: • five sentences • mixed lengths • more shorter sentences • caesura and enjambment stanza three: • one long sentence effect on rhythm stanza two: • otherwise regular rhythm broken • slows pace down (emphasises the smothering, quietening, numbing effect of the snow) effect on rhythm stanza three: • regular rhythm resumed (emphasises comfort of being inside/ emphasises movement resumed/ emphasises relentlessness of sleet)	4	award up to 2 marks for analysis of each stanza award up to 2 marks for explanation of the effects on the rhythm (candidate may go as far as to explain why the poet chose to manipulate the rhythms in this way)
5.	he likes/is interested in the features of sleet: • 'It was fine in the wind,' (line 3) – pretty and light	4	up to 4 marks for two reasons with quotation and explanation

	• 'dissolving spiders on cheekbones,' (line 9) – likes the feel of the pleasant, light touch • 'smudging the mind/That humped itself by the fire' (lines 10–11) – likes the feeling of lethargy and lazily slumping by the fire • 'turning away/From the ill wind' (lines 11–12) – excuse to go inside for shelter he finds the features of sleet all-consuming/ oppressive/depressing: • 'It swished heavily' (line 1) – claustrophobic flurry of falling sleet • 'It died a pauper's death.' (line 4) – just dies without having had a proper life • 'dissolving spiders on cheekbones' (line 9) – doesn't like the feel of the cold on the face • 'Being melted spit on the glass' (line 10) – leaves an unattractive residue on windows • 'smudging the mind/That humped itself by the fire' (lines 10–11) – doesn't like the feeling of confusion and lethargy • 'turning away/From the ill wind' (lines 11–12) – driven inside against his wish • 'the sky filthily weeping.' (line 12) – as if the sky is crying dirty tears/mirrors his depressed mood		reward other sensible suggestions
TOTAL		**25**	

9. Extract from 'The Rime of the Ancient Mariner' by Samuel Taylor Coleridge

Level 1

Q		Answer	Mark	Additional guidance
1.	(a)	• there are difficult weather conditions for the sailors/their boat becomes stuck in ice • their ship heads off course to the south	2	up to 2 marks for reference to bad weather/ice and ship off course/in difficulty
	(b)	• the arrival of the albatross • the sailors are pleased to see it as it follows them/helps them	2	up to 2 marks for reference to arrival/help of the albatross and sailors' reactions
2.	(a)	they are surrounded by ice/they are all alone in strange surroundings/have gone off course/are lost/the weather is extreme: • 'loud roared the blast' (line 1) • 'And now there came both mist and snow,' (line 3) • 'And it grew wondrous cold' (line 4) • 'And ice, mast-high came floating by' (line 5) • 'Nor shapes of men nor beasts we ken' (line 9) • 'The ice was all between' (line 10) • 'The ice was here, the ice was there,/ The ice was all around' (lines 11–12) • 'It cracked and growled, and roared and howled' (line 13)	3	1 mark for explanation of why worried 2 marks for two supporting quotations
	(b)	the conditions and weather get better/an albatross seems to help/guide them/they are able to continue their journey: • 'At length did cross an Albatross' (line 15) • 'As it had been a Christian soul' (line 17) • 'The ice did split with a thunder-fit' (line 21) • 'The helmsman steered us through!' (line 22) • 'And a good south wind sprung up behind' (line 23)	3	1 mark for explanation of why relieved 2 marks for two supporting quotations

		• 'The Albatross did follow' (line 24) • 'It perched for vespers nine' (line 28) • 'Glimmered the white moonshine.' (line 30)		
3.	(a)	'The ice was here, the ice was there,/ The ice was all around:' (lines 11–12) – repetition – emphasis of how much ice or similar	3	1 mark for quotation 1 mark for naming repetition 1 mark for effect
	(b)	• 'cracked', 'growled', 'roared', 'howled' *answers may refer to:* • enables you to hear the splintering of the ice • as if the ice is an angry creature • sounds of splintering ice magnified	3	1 mark for two examples of onomatopoeia 1 mark for effect
4.	(a)	• rhythm: 4 stresses, 3 stresses, 4 stresses, 3 stresses each stanza • rhyme: second and fourth lines rhyme abcd	2	rhythm: note stresses in stanzas for 1 mark rhyme: note second and fourth lines rhyming/or abcd in stanzas for 1 mark
	(b)	• moves it along fast • makes it pacey • makes it seems musical/songlike • gives it urgency • makes you want to keep reading • comforting/easy to read • comforting contrast with tension • reads to the ends of lines • seals the lines	2	two reasons needed
5.	(a)	• God/Heaven/or similar • split the ice (line 21) • good south wind (line 23) • stayed with them for nine days (line 28)	3	one needed for 1 mark two ways needed for 2 marks
	(b)	*answers may refer to:* • God/good fortune/safe travel/hope • trust in God • have faith • Christian belief that God will be a saviour	2	one symbol needed for 1 mark one sensible message needed for 1 mark
TOTAL			25	

104

9. Extract from 'The Rime of the Ancient Mariner' by Samuel Taylor Coleridge

Level 2

Q	Answer	Mark	Additional guidance
1.	• there are difficult weather conditions for the sailors/their boat becomes stuck in ice as their ship heads off course to the south • the arrival of the albatross and how the sailors are pleased to see it as it follows them/helps them by releasing them from the ice	2	up to 2 marks reward answers which indicate understanding of basic plot
2.	*answers may refer to:* threatened: • 'loud roared the blast' (line 1) – elements frightening desperate/despairing: • 'And ice, mast-high, came floating by' (line 5) – huge iceberg looms petrified: • 'Nor shapes of men nor beasts we ken' (line 9) – isolated/do not recognise anything/alone • 'growled', 'roared', ' howled' (line 13) – unfamiliar loud noises apprehensive: • 'And it grew wondrous cold' (line 4) – unbelievably cold/out of their experience fearful: • 'And southward aye we fled' (line 2) – going off course/out of control helpless: • 'The ice was all between' (line 10) – they are stuck and surrounded by ice happy/exultant: • 'As it had been a Christian soul' (line 17) – something familiar/living and good after previous troubles • 'The helmsman steered us through!' (line 22) – able to sail again	6	three emotions, plus supporting evidence and explanation necessary for 6 marks or two emotions with supporting evidence and explanation in more detail reward a response which selects contrasting emotions (emotions and quotations may be interchangeable)

	relieved/thankful/hopeful: • 'The ice did split with a thunder-fit' (line 21) – ice miraculously cracks and they are able to sail again optimistic: • 'We hailed it in God's name' (line 18) – hopeful that they will be saved • 'And a good south wind sprung up behind' (line 23) – beginning to sail fast again • 'Glimmered the white moonshine.' (line 30) – sky is clear again companionable: • 'for food or play,/Came to the mariner's hollo!' (lines 25–26) – enjoying the bird's company after previous loneliness/lifelessness		
3.	• 'And ice, mast-high' (line 5) – adjective – emphasises height and size • 'As green as emerald.' (line 6) – simile – bright and shining green • 'And through the drifts the snowy clifts' (line 7) – internal rhyme/assonance – draws the words closer together • 'Did send a dismal sheen' (line 8) – powerful adjective – light affected by their size • 'The ice was here, the ice was there,/The ice was all around' (lines 11–12) – repetition – emphasises how much ice – cluster/rule of three/three similar phrases for emphasis • 'cracked', 'growled,' 'roared', 'howled' (line 13) – onomatopoeia – enables you to hear the splintering of the ice/as if the ice is an angry creature • 'growled', 'howled' (line 13) – internal rhyme – emphasises sound • 'growled', 'roared', 'howled' (line 13) – metaphor – the ice is a noisy, angry creature • 'Like noises in a swound!' (line 14) – simile – as if sounds are blurred/distorted because of fainting/blackout	6	reward best/most relevant quotations technique/device to be named and effect explained each time two in more detail or three in less detail

4.	rhythm:	6	1 mark for recognising regularity
	• regular		2 marks if pattern of regularity identified
	• 4 stresses, 3 stresses, 4 stresses, 3 stresses in the four-line stanzas		
	rhyme:		1 mark for recognising regularity
	• regular second and fourth lines rhyme abcb		2 marks if pattern of regularity identified
	• moves it along fast		2 marks for two sensible suggestions
	• makes it pacey		
	• makes it seems musical/song-like		(the effect of rhythm and rhyme may be dealt with separately or together)
	• gives it urgency		
	• makes you want to keep reading		
	• comforting/easy to read		
	• comforting contrast with tension		
	rhyme:		
	• go to the ends of lines		
	• seals the lines		
5. (a)	• their fortunes/weather change:	4	up to 2 marks for relevant and sensible suggestions
	• splits the ice (line 21)		
	• good south wind (line 23)		
	• albatross stays with them for nine days (line 27)		
(b)	• God	1	up to 2 marks for relevant and sensible suggestions
	• good fortune		
	• safe travel		
	• hope		
	• or similar		
	answers may refer to:		reward any sensible suggestion
	• trust in God		
	• have faith		
	• Christian belief that God will be a saviour		
TOTAL		**25**	

10. 'Silence' by Thomas Hood

Level 1

Q		Answer	Mark	Additional guidance
1.		line 1: • the silence is because there has never been a sound line 2: • the silence is because there never will/cannot be a sound	2	1 mark for understanding each type of silence
2.	(a)	• 'In the cold grave' (line 3) • 'under the deep, deep sea,' (line 3) • 'in wide desert where no life is found' (line 4)	3	1 mark for each
	(b)	• 'in green ruins' (line 9) • 'in the desolate walls/Of antique palaces' (lines 9–10)	2	1 mark for each
3.		• 'deep, deep sea' (line 3) • 'no life' (line 4), 'No voice' (line 6), 'no life' (line 6) • 'deep, deep sea' – emphasises depth of sea • 'no life' (line 4), 'no life' (line 6) – emphasises that nothing is living in the desert • 'No voice' (line 6), 'no life' (line 6) – emphasises that there are no creatures/people there to create a sound or movement	4	up to 2 marks for two examples of repetition two examples of 'no' repetition sufficient up to 2 marks for understanding of use of repetition for emphasis
4.		• 'Shriek' (line 13), 'moan' (line 13) • 'Shriek' (line 13) – the effect is that the reader can hear the high-pitched/anguished cries of the fox, hyaena, owls/animals • 'moan' (line 13) – the effect is that the reader can hear the sad/low/mournful cry of the wind	2 4	1 mark for each correct identification up to 2 marks, each time, for effect of word on reader and explanation

5.	(a)	lines 9–12: • there is a rhyme on alternate lines	1	1 mark for identifying rhyme pattern
	(b)	lines 13–14: • they rhyme with each other/rhyming couplet	1	1 mark for identifying rhyme pattern
		• the last two lines are linked together for a powerful ending • to make the last two lines important • the sounds you are left with are long, low and depressing	2	up to 2 marks for sensible responses
6.		• he feels that the silence where people once were is emphasised/stronger/more powerful because it is a sadder/more lonely sort of silence because there used to be sound there	4	marker's discretion up to 4 marks for understanding of the nature of the silence in places where people had once been/some understanding of the poet's message
TOTAL			**25**	

10. 'Silence' by Thomas Hood

Level 2

Q		Answer	Mark	Additional guidance
1.	(a)	• there is a silence where there has never been any sound • there is a silence where there will never/ cannot be a sound	2	both lines to be explained
	(b)	• silent places lines 3–4: grave/sea/desert • silent places lines 9–10: ruins/walls of palaces contrast: • grave/sea/desert – never has been life there/natural/inaccessible places • ruins/palaces – man-made/once contained life	4	up to 2 marks for identifying places up to 2 marks for recognising contrast
2.		• 'There is a silence…' (lines 1 and 2) – emphasises the theme of the poem/ points out that there are two sorts of silence • 'no sound' (lines 1 and 2) – no sound in either place • 'deep, deep sea' (line 3) – emphasises depth of sea • 'no' (lines 1, 2, 4 and 6) – nothing at all can be heard • 'no life' (lines 4 and 6), – emphasises that nothing is living in the desert • 'No voice' (line 6), 'no life' (line 6) – emphasises that there are no creatures/ people there to create a sound or movement	4	up to 4 marks for two explained examples of repetition
3.		atmosphere: lonely/bleak/eerie/depressing: • 'desolate walls/Of antique palaces' (lines 9–10) – personification – the walls have been abandoned by people • 'wild hyaena calls' (line 11)/'owls, that flit' (line 12) – vocabulary choices emphasise the desolate environment – the loneliness	6	up to 6 marks for recognition of atmosphere, supported by explained examples of words/poetic techniques

	is extending from a place to now include wild/mysterious creatures • 'Shriek' (line 13) – onomatopoeia – high-pitched/anguished cries of the fox, hyaena, owls/animals • 'moan' (line 13) – onomatopoeia – the sad/low/mournful cry of the wind – the eerie sounds add to the desolate picture		reference to 'sustained' atmosphere could be explained throughout or explained at the end
4.	first change in pattern: line 9 from abba to cdcd second change in pattern: line 13 from cdcd to ee – rhyming couplet • first change signifies change in meaning/content/poet's thoughts: from writing about the silence that is found in silent places where there never has been/never will or cannot be sound to writing about silent places which have previously been inhabited • second change signifies a linking together of the last two lines for a powerful ending/to emphasise the end of the poem/to emphasise the long, sustained, low, depressing sounds ('moan' and 'alone') • first change is because, in some sonnet forms, the rhyme scheme changes between the octet and the sestet • second change is because, in some sonnet forms, the final two lines display a rhyming couplet	5	up to 2 marks for identifying where or how the rhyme patterns change up to 3 marks for sensible reasons which explain significance of changes candidates are not expected to have knowledge of sonnet form, but reward them if they do
5.	• the poet feels that the silence in places which were once inhabited is a more real/powerful silence • this is emphasised by the capital letter ('Silence') • the silence experienced in these places is more disturbing/uncomfortable/worrying ('self-conscious') as there is a sadness in now silent places which have once been filled with the sounds of people	4	marker's discretion award marks for an understanding of the poet's message, to include analysis of specific vocabulary

	• the loneliness ('alone') in these places is accentuated/exaggerated as once they were filled with the sounds of people which contrasts with the present silence • even though there may be the sounds of creatures in these places, they do not make up for/but emphasise the lack of human sounds		
TOTAL		**25**	

Paper 1 Section B:
Writing for a practical purpose
ISEB descriptors

Paper 1 Essays 1–3 (and Paper 2 essays)

Mark	Descriptors
1–11	Not relevant to the chosen task; clarity weak owing to poor organisation and technical inaccuracy; very short and undeveloped with little attention to detail.
12–15	Generally relevant to the task; ideas clearly communicated and organised into paragraphs; some attention to detail; style and tone generally appropriate for the chosen task; spelling sufficiently accurate.
16–19	Mainly relevant to the task; ideas clearly communicated and well structured in an effective and interesting way; good attention to detail; style and tone adapted well for the chosen task; spelling generally accurate; a good range of vocabulary and expression.
20–25	Consistently relevant to the task; ideas developed fully and well structured in an original and stylish way; excellent attention to detail; essay much enhanced by style and tone; spelling consistently accurate; a wide range of vocabulary and expression.

Essay titles 1–3 in Paper 1 Section B provide the candidate with the opportunity to write for a practical purpose: to argue, persuade, explain, advise or inform.

Guidelines to aid interpretation of key words in descriptors

Relevance

The essay must be based on the given title with appropriate reference to it.

The purpose of the chosen genre should be adhered to in style, content and tone.

Ideas

Ideas within the essay should be thought provoking, engaging and, if relevant, informative and original.

Structure

The structure of the essay should show evidence of clear planning and sequencing of ideas.

Paragraph breaks should be used purposefully and the progression of ideas within each paragraph should be fluent.

Topic sentences should be used clearly at the beginning of each paragraph with ensuing ideas clearly grouped.

The use of discourse pointers is important to enable the reader to understand the direction of the writing.

A strong opening and conclusion should be evident.

Letter writing: the correct placing and spacing of addresses, date and sign-off is expected.

The structure of argument and persuasive writing has specific requirements:

Argument writing

Argument writing should provide an introduction to outline the topic, followed by clear and balanced paragraphs for and against the topic and a conclusion where the writer's opinion may be given.

Persuasive writing

Persuasive writing should provide an arresting opening followed by logical and paragraphed ideas dealing largely with one side of the argument. The conclusion should leave the reader in no doubt as to the opinion of the writer/speaker.

Detail

A clear understanding and knowledge of the subject matter should underpin the writing.

Points should be well-explained, with supporting evidence or anecdotal reference where appropriate.

Style

The candidate's grasp of grammar and syntax should be clear and confident.

Sentence structures should provide a variety of openings; simple, compound and complex sentences should be used appropriately and smoothly according to the context.

Verb tenses should be used accurately and consistently.

Argument writing

Argument writing should mainly be written in the passive tense to provide objectivity.

A range of persuasive writing techniques should be evident but used in a moderate way.

Persuasive writing

Persuasive writing should be written in the active and imperative tenses to convey subjectivity.

A wide range of persuasive writing techniques/features should be evident and used in a forceful or persuasive way.

Writing to explain, advise, inform

These genres of writing may require the use of present, conditional or modal tenses.

Tone

The tone and degree of formality should be appropriate to the genre, purpose, subject matter and audience.

The use of a humorous tone should be measured and acceptable to all readers.

Spelling

Genre and subject-specific words should be spelt accurately.

Vocabulary

An interesting and sophisticated vocabulary, specific to the genre, should be used.

Paper 1 Section B:
Writing on a literary topic
ISEB descriptors

Paper 1 Essay 4 (literary topic)

Mark	Descriptors
1–11	Knowledge and understanding of the text(s) not relevant to the task; not clear in terms of organisation; technically very inaccurate; very short and undeveloped.
12–15	Knowledge and understanding of the text(s) generally relevant to the task; some reference to the text made to support ideas; ideas clearly communicated and organised into paragraphs; spelling sufficiently accurate.
16–19	Knowledge and understanding of the text(s) mainly relevant to the task; good reference to the text to develop ideas; ideas clearly communicated; well-structured essay; spelling generally accurate.
20–25	Knowledge and understanding of the text(s) consistently relevant to the task; sound insight shown; close reference to the text to develop ideas fully; ideas clearly communicated; detailed and well-structured essay; spelling generally accurate; a good range of appropriate vocabulary.

The fourth essay title/question in Paper 1 Section B is a choice of two literary topics. These provide the candidate with the opportunity to write in detail on a given subject in a chosen text, which might include moments of drama, transition, contrast and various other ideas.

Guidelines to aid interpretation of key words in descriptors

Knowledge

Essays should display knowledge of the text: plot, characters, setting(s), historical context and possibly author's background.

Understanding

Candidates should be able to sift relevant information and apply understanding and insight to the chosen essay question.

Relevance to the task

An accurate understanding of the question must be proved: constant reference to the demands of the question should be evident. Candidates should take care not simply to retell the story.

Reference to text

Relevant examples from the chosen text should be used to explain and support statements and ideas. Care should be taken to include detailed examples yet without irrelevant information.

Ideas clearly communicated

Ideas should be clearly communicated in a convincing way. Candidates should plan carefully and guide the marker confidently through a well-shaped and logical essay.

Structure

The structure of the essay should show evidence of clear planning and sequencing of ideas.

The introduction should state the book(s) and author(s) studied and prove an understanding of the demands of the question.

The main body of the essay should develop a logical and clear progression of ideas with supporting evidence and, at all times, directly answer the question.

Paragraph breaks should be used purposefully and the progression of ideas within each paragraph should be fluent.

Topic sentences should be used clearly at the beginning of each paragraph with ensuing ideas clearly grouped.

Careful use of discourse pointers will enable the reader to follow and understand the interpretation of the question.

The conclusion will summarise and emphasise the preceding key points.

Spelling

Spelling should be generally accurate with due care given to words specific to the book, to include the characters and places. The correct spelling and punctuation of the book and author is assumed.

Vocabulary

Candidates should display a confident range of vocabulary.

Paper 2 Section B:
Writing to provoke imaginative, descriptive or narrative responses
ISEB descriptors

Paper 2 Essays (and Paper 1 Essays 1–3)

Mark	Descriptors
1–11	Not relevant to the chosen task; clarity weak owing to poor organisation and technical inaccuracy; very short and undeveloped with little attention to detail.
12–15	Generally relevant to the task; ideas clearly communicated and organised into paragraphs; some attention to detail; style and tone generally appropriate for the chosen task; spelling sufficiently accurate.
16–19	Mainly relevant to the task; ideas clearly communicated and well structured in an effective and interesting way; good attention to detail; style and tone adapted well for the chosen task; spelling generally accurate; a good range of vocabulary and expression.
20–25	Consistently relevant to the task; ideas developed fully and well structured in an original and stylish way; excellent attention to detail; essay much enhanced by style and tone; spelling consistently accurate; a wide range of vocabulary and expression.

Fiction writing skills, imaginative, descriptive or narrative, are here dealt with separately, despite the above descriptors being the same as for writing for a practical purpose.

Relevance

The essay must be based on the given title with appropriate reference to it.

The genre chosen should be adhered to in style, content and tone.

Ideas

Ideas should reflect a creative and original use and interpretation of the title.

Structure

The structure of the essay should show clear planning and sequencing of ideas.

Paragraph breaks should be used purposefully and the progression of ideas within each paragraph should be fluent.

Imaginative

Imaginative writing will fall into the descriptive or narrative genres.

Narrative

The overall shape of the story should be clear and evident, with a strong opening and with a purposeful end in mind.

It could embrace the use of flashback or other stylistic devices.

Candidates should show off their ability to write an interesting and manageable plot with appropriate crisis and shape.

There should be sufficient balance between the plot, the description of the characters within it and the setting.

Descriptive

The structure of descriptive writing should be clearly evident. For example, the writer's viewpoint, if describing a place, should be established: whether describing a landscape in an organised way from a static position or as if passing through it. Similarly, there are various ways to structure the description of a character or object and care should be taken to ensure that the piece is not disjointed and that ideas are clearly connected.

Detail

The ability to focus on, and write with, sufficient detail will engage the reader and ensure that the writing is not mainly 'plot driven'.

The reader needs to be able to picture his/her surroundings: appropriate setting details may range from the overview, such as weather and light, to the immediate foreground.

To provide this detail the setting(s) could be explored through a variety of senses.

Characters should be developed in a detailed way, to go beyond physical attributes and to include consistent and believable actions, dialogue, reactions and feelings. Care should be taken not to over-use dialogue.

If the chosen writing genre is descriptive, the detail should be greatly enhanced.

Style

The candidate's grasp of grammar and syntax should be clear and confident. Best candidates will be in command of language and may present an individual voice and personal flair.

Sentence structures should provide a variety of openings: simple, compound and complex sentences should be used appropriately and smoothly according to the context.

Verb tenses should be used accurately and consistently and tense changes used for effect where appropriate.

A range of writing features such as imagery, sound devices and the powerful use of vocabulary should be used to enhance the composition. These should be particularly evident in descriptive writing.

Tone

The tone should enhance the writing and should be appropriate to the genre and audience.

Care should be taken with the use of violence, adult issues and innuendo.

The use of a humorous tone should be measured and acceptable to all readers.

Spelling

Spelling should be generally accurate but candidates should not be penalised for misspelling adventurous and sophisticated words.

Vocabulary

A sophisticated, relevant and succinct vocabulary will set apart best candidates.

The use of inappropriate slang and modern euphemisms should be avoided.